5 Star Reviews for Recent North/Goetsch Books

American Gulags: Marxist Tyranny in Higher Education and What to Do About It—9781956454062—May 24, 2023

Jenn Parker

What is Really Going On in Schools and Universities

"This is a must read book for anyone that cares about the education system in the United States. It is now an indoctrination system that thinks it owns our children and wants them at the preschool age so they can control their beliefs. It is no longer a public education system that seeks to teach our kids and help them excel, they now teach to the lowest common denominator. The current government indoctrination system is planned and designed and is not an accident. Parents MUST get involved and protect our kids from the Marxist indoctrination they are now exposed to."

Sandra Johnson

Awesome Book

"Oliver North as a very high ranking Marine, has been a very valuable asset to the USA throughout his extensive career. He knows exactly what's going on with the indoctrination of our kids in schools. He explains this serious situation in full and also explains what we can do to stop it, protecting our kids and our country."

Reading Renee

Fantastic book Eye opener

"What a fantastic book. American parents need to be aware of useless degree programs, socialist behaviors and kids joining in on them while being unaware of the consequences. Colonel North who is highly decorated, explains the traps that kids can be put into. College is a learning experience and shouldn't be about some of these agendas.

"I'm so glad I read this."

Trance Dancer

How Universities Breed Hate and Division

"An intimate and concise expose of the evolution of Marxism in Higher Education which has led to rampant antisemitism, lack of patriotism, class warfare and a racial divide. The same type kids that turned in their parents to the Nazi's are the same type of kids that support a one world progressive Government 'to take care of them'"

Tragic Consequences: The Price America is Paying for Rejecting God and How to Reclaim Our Culture for Christ—9781956454000—May 18, 2022

TGyr

Makes Sense

"I am reading this book now. It makes sense to me. I hope more people will read it."

Paul

Great insight.

"North nails America's greatest problem and what the consequences are. Easy and understandable read."

Unnamed reader

Need to read

"If you're concerned about the way things are g
an eye opener."

T0283823

Kristi

A Must-Read For All!

"*Tragic Consequences* is one of the best books I have ever read, and should be required reading for all. Brilliantly written, with deep insight, courage and love. Analyzes what has gone wrong in our country, and how we can work to save it, on six fronts: the family, church, education, politics, the courtroom, and the public square. Please share this urgently needed book with everyone you know."

Cathy Hugick

GREAT READ AND FACTUAL

"This book is to the point and very insightful in the crazy world of today. Read it and learn the real truth about how things are! Go back to Christ and relook at the world as it is!"

Maggie L

So true

"God bless LT COL Oliver North. He speaks the truth. This is a God send. I salute and thank you Sir . . . . Great book. God bless you. A must read.

"Peace."

Eve Rivera

This book is a great blessing and a must-read for all true Christian believers !!

"We liked the factual and Biblically-based comments of the authors—something that only those who read and follow God's Word as a way of life can know."

Gene Skrobarcek

Getting to the root cause of our social decline.

"That the author took on what others knew, but were afraid to say for fear of reprisals."

W. Frank Agee

Good Book

"This should be a must read by anyone interested in American History."

gebeaver

Rejection of Godly values

"right on target as to why USA is in a moral decline"

Ronald A Feaster

Required reading

"This book should be required reading in all schools through out America. Call it a history book with the founding fathers belief system explained. If the education establishment (NEA) doesn't like it . . . tough."

Karen

Great book!

"Truth!!"

OLIVER L. NORTH
AND DAVID L. GOETSCH

THINK
IT OVER

HOW TO USE CRITICAL THINKING TO AVOID FALSITY AND FAILURE

FIDELIS PUBLISHING ®

ISBN: 9781956454536
ISBN (eBook): 9781956454543

Think It Over
How to Use Critical Thinking to Avoid Falsity and Failure
© 2024 Oliver L. North and David L. Goetsch

Cover Design by Diana Lawrence
Interior Design by Xcel Graphic
Edited by Amanda Varian

Order at www.faithfultext.com for a significant discount. Email info@fidelis publishing.com to inquire about bulk purchase discounts.

All Scripture paraphrastically quoted.

Individuals named herein are fictional. Any similarity to actual people is unintentional.

Fidelis Publishing, LLC Sterling, VA • Nashville, TN
fidelispublishing.com

Manufactured in the United States of America

10 9 8 7 6 5 4 3 2 1

But the old sceptic, the complete sceptic says,
"I have no right to think for myself,
I have no right to think at all."

—G. K. Chesterton (1874–1936)
from *Orthodoxy* (1908)

CONTENTS

INTRODUCTION

*O*ur country is being torn apart by chaos, turmoil, violence, and political division. Riots, arson, looting, smash-and-grab burglaries, mass shootings, and cultural clashes are now commonplace. Traditional American values are declining. Patriotism, religion, and family have become less important than in the past and, to many, unimportant. The dominant American culture has become narcissistic and hedonistic. In our history, one of the most cherished American values was the truth. When people dealt with dilemmas, issues, opinions, and decisions, their first question was "What is the truth in this situation?" Now people are concerned only with what they think, feel, and want. We have lost touch with the importance of truth in our lives.

Because of self-serving concerns, such as "I think, I feel and I want," many people are willing to lie, distort, and deceive to get their way. As a result, you are being lied to everyday. The lies come from politicians, professors, teachers, advertisers, media outlets, coworkers, fellow students, friends, and even family members. This is why it is so important that you become a critical thinker—an objective reasoner who can separate truth from fiction in what you are told, hear, and observe.

For example, in business, being a critical thinker can lead to better decisions and more effective solutions. This, in turn, leads to better efficiency, quality, and productivity. Critical thinking is good for business and it is good for every other field of human endeavor. Think about some of the prominent business failures you may have heard of. They include New Century

Financial Corporation, Wirecard AG, Bank of New England Corporation, Blockbuster, Enron, BlackBerry, Kodak, Pan Am Airline, First Republic Bank, Silicon Valley Bank, and Polaroid to name just a few. There are many more failures from the world of business as well as other fields caused by the same problem. What these failed businesses all have in common is they nose-dived because they failed to think critically about how changes in markets, technology, and other evolving factors would affect them. As a result, they failed to innovate.

An attitude of I think, I feel, and I want leads to failures that grow out of deception, distortion, and lies leading inevitably to bad decisions which, in turn, lead to failure. Here are just a few examples of how you are lied to regularly.

- Politicians tell you they can continue spending your tax dollars recklessly without putting our nation's future at risk.
- Professors who have never lived in a Marxist nation tell you socialism is superior to democracy and capitalism in spite of the horrible conditions characterizing life in socialist countries. The millions of illegal immigrants flooding across America's southern border attest to the conditions in socialist countries.
- Teachers tell you, as a parent, you have no say in what your children are taught. They also tell you they should be able to guide your children to sex change operations without your involvement or consent.
- Advertisers hype their products without regard to the actual quality, performance, or benefits of the products, emphasizing the upside while hiding, disguising, or minimizing the downside. How many ads for prescriptions drugs have you seen recently?
- Media outlets have become mouthpieces for the political party of their choice. As a result, they twist the news to suit their agendas while telling you they report the truth.

- Coworkers take credit for the good work of colleagues and point the finger of blame at others when they have failed.
- Fellow students cheat on assignments and tests but claim otherwise.
- Friends tell you "little white lies" to keep from hurting your feelings.
- Family members sometimes lie to get their way in family discussions. As an example, you want eggs and bacon for breakfast, but your sister, whose turn it is to cook, wants you to eat cereal. She claims the family is out of eggs when, in fact, there are plenty of eggs in the refrigerator.

All these lies are told to help the liars get what they think, want, or feel. The liars have no regard for truth. When we lose sight of truth, society breaks down and we end up with the chaos, turmoil, violence, and political divisions now undermining the nation our Founders envisioned. But you do not have to be lied to. You can recognize and reject lies, distortion, and deception by becoming a critical thinker. The key is to learn the critical thinking skills presented in this book.

These skills include recognizing bias, evaluating motives, distinguishing between facts and opinions, distinguishing between explanations and rationalizations, researching the facts, distinguishing between real solutions and short-term expedients, separating issues from opinions, applying common sense, rejecting ad hominem arguments, refusing to ignore uncomfortable facts, rejecting oversimplification, and rejecting distorted conclusions. *Think It Over* will teach you all these skills.

1

WHAT IS CRITICAL THINKING AND WHY IS IT IMPORTANT?

*H*ave you ever been lied to? Most of us have. When you were lied to, how did it make you feel? For most people, being lied to is a decidedly negative experience. We feel like we've been betrayed, the rug has been pulled out from under us, and trust has been broken. This can often lead us to finding it hard to trust anyone. We all want to be able to trust those we interact with whether they are family members, friends, coworkers, fellow students, teachers, professors, politicians, or businesses.

Being unable to trust others leaves us adrift in a world of ambiguity where nothing is certain and nothing can be counted on. It is not uncommon to hear wives of husbands who have cheated on them say, "The lie he told to cover up the affair hurt worse than the affair." If we are paying attention, we are lied to everyday—not a comforting thought. Have you ever met an individual who liked being lied to? Probably not. We do not like being lied to. Fortunately, we do not have to be. We can stop others from lying to us. How? By learning to be a critical thinker.

WHAT IS CRITICAL THINKING?

Critical thinking is a process whereby we apply logic, reason, and common sense in interpreting, analyzing, and evaluating information we receive from any source. The point of critical thinking is to discover the truth. Critical thinkers are so committed to the truth, you might say they are addicted to it if, by addicted, we mean they will not settle for less. We receive information every day through observation and listening, not all of it accurate and not all of it truthful. Because of this, critical thinkers never accept information they receive at face value. Rather, they run it through an intellectual filter that involves calling on their experience, common sense, reason, logic, and, often, research.

The most successful people are critical thinkers. They know things are not always what they appear on the surface, advice is not always good, and information may not be accurate. They understand people will lie. They know failing to think critically can lead to mistakes, bad decisions, disputes, and broken relationships. In life, critical thinking can be the difference between success and failure. Ill-advised assumptions, biased input, and inaccurate information can lead to decisions that not only fail to produce the desired result, but actually make the situation worse.

Consider the example of the rookie businessman just out of college who has not yet traveled on airlines. Wondering how early he needs to show up for check-in, he asks a colleague for advice. The colleague tells him, "Forget what you hear about showing up two hours early. I never arrive at the check-in counter more than ten minutes early." Rather than think critically about this advice and doing some research, the rookie takes it at face value and misses his flight.

Here is another example. Pharmaceutical companies flood the air waves—television and the internet—with ads designed to convince you to buy their products or, better yet, have your insurance company pay. They often pay a popular actor to, with practiced sincerity, extol the virtues of their drug. Rather than accept the ad's claim at face value, you do some quick research on the internet and find the drug is not only poorly reviewed by actual users, but the side effects are worse than the problem the drug purports to solve. Those side effects are often listed at the end of the ad by a chirpy-voiced actor who can make dying sound like a happy experience. Unfortunately, by this time you have probably already fallen prey to the drug and its negative side effects.

Before going any further, we need to offer a clarification concerning the label "critical thinking." Thinking critically does not mean being a grouchy person who constantly criticizes others. However, in today's culture of emotion we have become so averse to hurting the feelings of others the term *critical* has taken on negative connotations. However, as has been the case repeatedly over the last few decades, we reject the Left's bending and breaking of the English language as a part of their strategy to control every narrative. So, we will stick with the phrase critical thinking in this book.

The meaning does not change. To be a critical thinker is to be an objective thinker. Objective thinking is a lack of bias or favoritism in seeking the truth in any given situation. Critical thinkers seek the truth independent of the subjectivity derived from bias, favoritism, or agendas. Further, they follow that truth wherever it leads, even when doing so is uncomfortable, inconvenient, or at odds with their personal preferences. An example of being rational is an individual trying to prove his or her opinion is correct, but learns it is not. A rational person puts aside the inaccurate opinion no matter how strongly he or she feels about it. That is the product of critical thinking.

WHY IS CRITICAL THINKING SO IMPORTANT?

Critical thinking is important because the truth is important. Why? Truth is important because it provides accurate information on which to base decisions or analyze the information we hear, read, and observe. Think about people who lie. Once they tell the first lie, they must continue lying to cover up each successive lie. This is the basis of the saying "what a tangled web we weave when, at first, we practice to deceive." Something aspiring critical thinkers should remember is this: If it's true, it's true no matter how many people deny it, and if it's false it's false no matter how many people believe it.

Believing what is not true can lead to problems large and small. There can even be legal and social consequences for lying. But telling the truth, no matter how inconvenient, will cause people to respect you—even liars. It also encourages them to be truthful with you. Telling the truth can establish powerful bonds and deep personal relationships making your life more rewarding, more significant, and more enjoyable. Honest people are trustworthy and loyal while liars tend to be greedy, unethical, and immoral.

Consider this example. Whenever John found himself struggling with telling the truth, he called on his friend Jake. No matter what the issue might be and no matter how difficult the truth might seem, Jake counseled John to tell the truth. Jake told John many times, "Even if the person you lie to never finds out, you know. Who wants to carry that burden."

WHY PEOPLE LIE

Here is a bit of bad news. People are going to lie to you. The obvious question is why? People lie for a number of different reasons, most of which are self-serving. People lie to avoid punishment, claiming "I didn't do it," when, in fact, they did. They also lie to avoid embarrassment, feed their ego by making themselves look important or heroic, pacify or appease others, sell you something you don't need, and to get attention, sympathy, or rewards. One of the most common reasons people lie is to push a personal, political, or business agenda. Finally, some people lie to avoid hurting the feelings of others.

A man we will call Stuart told friends and anyone else who would listen he was a combat decorated veteran of the Viet Nam War. He claimed to have earned the Silver Star and Purple Heart. Among his friends, Stuart was viewed as a hero. He was frequently invited to speak at veterans' events and other occasions honoring the military. Then, one day a reporter who interviewed him did some research and learned Stuart never served in the military. When his perfidy was exposed, Stuart's friends felt betrayed. They were lied to by someone they viewed as a hero. The reporter who exposed his lies turned him in and Stuart was charged with violating the Stolen Valor Act.

People will lie to avoid hurting the feelings of others. This happens when, for example, they claim to like a dress they, in truth, think looks terrible, say they enjoyed a meal they practically had to choke down, or say "you did a good job" when this is obviously not the case. The problem is when someone who has been told one of these so-called little *white lies* to avoid hurt feelings finds out the truth—which often happens—they feel worse than had you told the truth in the first place. They feel like a fool for trusting your words. Remember this: a little white lie is still a lie. People who tell little white lies will also tell whoppers when it suits their purpose.

METHODS LIARS USE TO COVER THEIR FALSITIES

Part of being a critical thinker is understanding liars will go to great lengths to cover their falsitys. It is important to recognize and reject these attempts by liars to conceal their lies. Their methods include using inflammatory language, appealing to compassion, using intimidating language, and using ridicule.

USING INFLAMMATORY LANGUAGE

Liars often try to divert attention from their lies by using inflammatory language. For example, assume you and your fellow members of a college fraternity are considering inviting Mike to join your club. One of the members says, "No way! I had a class with Mike. He will be lucky to graduate. He is a loser." Mike is actually an excellent student. The dissenting fraternity member is jealous of Mike's academic prowess. The inflammatory language brands Mike in a powerfully negative way because the fraternity in question maintains high academic standards for its members.

APPEALING TO COMPASSION

Liars sometimes appeal to compassion to make you sympathetic to their opinion, point of view, or agenda. For example, assume you are a supervisor at work and are considering two employees for promotion to an open position. One of your team members stops by your office and says, "I hope you will consider Susan for this promotion. You know she is a single mother. She needs the money. Medical bills for her daughter are really piling up."

You are sympathetic but decide to investigate before deciding on the promotion. It turns out Susan's daughter is not even sick. In fact, she is a healthy and thriving member of her high school's track team. The team member who falsely appealed to your compassion is dating Susan and lied to improve her chances of getting the promotion.

USING INTIMIDATING LANGUAGE

Liars sometimes use intimidating language to scare you into accepting their lies. For example, Margaret is the mother of twins who attend the local elementary school. She is concerned about the school's new class in critical race theory (CRT). Recently, one of her sons came home from school and asked, "Mom, why do we oppress minorities?" Margaret considered going to a school board meeting and speaking out against the teaching of CRT, but before deciding she talked with a neighbor whose children also attend the local elementary school.

Her neighbor, unbeknownst to Margaret, is a supporter of teaching CRT. To deter Margaret, the neighbor says, "I wouldn't speak to the school board if I were you. You might get arrested as a domestic terrorist." In reality, the school board received numerous complaints from parents and was considering dropping the CRT course. Unfortunately, the intimidating language served its purpose. Margaret decided not to attend a school board meeting.

USING RIDICULE

Liars will sometimes use ridicule to embarrass you into going along with their lies. For example, assume you are trying to make an important decision about where to go to college. You have a scholarship to your local university but are concerned about stories of anti-Christian attitudes on campus. As a result, you are considering attending an out-of-state Christian university that will cost much more in tuition and fees. You decide to speak with a counselor at your hometown university.

When you explain your concerns, he says, "You are going to look ridiculous if you go to an out-of-state university when you have a scholarship to attend here. People are going to think you have lost your mind. Besides, the rumors of anti-Christian attitudes are just that, rumors." Sensitive to looking ridiculous, you enroll at the local university only to find the rumors of anti-Christian attitudes are not just true but understated. In fact, it is much worse even as I write, campuses are overrun by bloodthirsty zealots demanding the extermination of Jews.

YOUR TRUTH IS NOT MY TRUTH

In today's woke culture, ideologues who claim boys not old enough to cross the street on their own can decide to be girls, without their parents' involvement or permission, the truth is being viewed as relative. Non-rational thinkers are fond of claiming, "What is true for you may not be true for me." That may well be the case regarding how one likes their steak cooked, but beyond such preferences, "relative" truth is nonsense. To woke ideologues, truth is whatever they decide it is; whatever serves their purpose in the moment. What they consider true today they might consider false tomorrow depending on their whims. The problems with this distorted and agenda-driven belief system are so obvious a child could point them out.

To claim someone can decide what is true is to make that individual into a god. The hubris required to claim "I can decide what is true" is outside sane thinking. People, no matter how ideologically driven, are not gods, and the truth is not relative. It is unerring, unchanging, unalterable, and infallible. The truth can be hard to accept, but it has the power to improve lives, encourage people to love each other, change individuals for the better, and protect against destructive ideologies.

If people can decide what is true, what happens when their truth clashes with someone else's truth. The answer is chaos and conflict, which is where we are in our country today. All the chaos and conflict surrounding such controversies as men identifying as women so as to unfairly compete in women's athletics, Critical Race Theory (CRT), transgenderism, mistrust of government, abortion, and other cultural issues are caused by one thing: denial by woke ideologues of the truth.

LEARNING TO BE A CRITICAL THINKER

There is a lot of bad news presented in this chapter, but don't despair. Here is some good news. You can learn to be a critical thinker able to recognize when you are being lied to and act accordingly. The remainder of this book is a series of how-to chapters that teach critical thinking skills. Once you have developed the skills taught in the remainder of this book, you will never have to worry about being the victim of lies again. You will still be lied to, there is no doubt about that. But now you will be able to recognize and reject the lies. More good news is the more you practice thinking objectively the easier it gets.

Alonzo is a critical thinker. He knows finding the truth is the ultimate goal when discussing and debating issues. One day in a college class, the professor was lecturing on the relativity of truth. He claimed the truth is a manmade concept determined by the circumstances of the moment and the preferences of those involved. Alonzo raised his hand and asked, "Are you saying there is no such thing as absolute truth?" The professor responded, "That is precisely what I am saying."

Alonzo asked the professor if he ever disagreed with someone who also thinks the truth is relative. The professor said he had but did not accept their views as truth. Alonzo then asked the professor how he settled the argument. The professor said "we didn't." Alonzo asked the professor, "Is that because you had no basis for settling?" The professor, red faced and addled, replied, "Let's move on to another topic."

SUMMARY

- Critical thinking is applying logic, reason, experience, and common sense in analyzing and evaluating information we hear, read, or observe. Critical thinkers never accept input at face value. Rather, they run it though an intellectual filter that involves calling on their experience, common sense, reason, logic, and, often, research.
- The most important aspect of critical thinking is it requires the application of wisdom. Wisdom means seeking the truth and applying it in analyzing the information we know or can discover through research.
- Critical thinking is important because the truth is important and critical thinking involves seeking the truth. Accepting

what is not true—accepting lies—leads to problems large and small.

- People lie for a number of reasons, all of which are self-serving. People lie to avoid blame and punishment, avoid embarrassment, feed their egos, appease others, sell you something you don't need, and garner attention, sympathy, or rewards.
- Methods liars use to cover their falsitiess include using inflammatory language, appealing to compassion, using intimidating language, and using ridicule.
- People who apply the "I think, I feel, and I want" model believe—or at least claim—truth is relative. It can be determined by individuals based on the situation and the preferences of the individuals involved.
- You can learn to be a critical thinker able to recognize when you are being lied to. Once you have developed critical thinking skills, you will never again have to worry about being misled by lies. You will still be lied to; there is no doubt about that, but with critical thinking skills you will be able to recognize and reject the lies and the damage they inflict.

2

BEHAVIORS CRITICAL THINKERS MUST AVOID

Critical thinking is not a skill we are born with. Rather, it must be learned, developed, and practiced constantly. The first step in becoming a critical thinker has two parts. First, it is important to recognize when you are dealing with people who lie, distort, and deceive. The second step is to avoid the same behaviors. Do not be like the people who hope you will not think objectively.

Lying to people allows them to justify in their own dishonest hearts lying to you. Their reasoning goes like this: "If he is going to lie to me, why shouldn't I lie to him?" The principle behind avoiding non-rational thinking behaviors is biblical. It comes from Matthew 7:5 where we are told to take the log out of our own eye before we concern ourselves with the speck in our neighbor's eye.

IRRATIONAL THINKING BEHAVIORS TO AVOID

If you find yourself beginning to exhibit irrational thinking behaviors, it is important to recognize it and make a quick correction. Behaviors critical thinkers must recognize and reject in others while also avoiding them include the following:

- Being closed-minded, inflexible, and stubborn when discussing issues and opinions
- Being too receptive and too willing to accept any opinion
- Being arrogant and overly confident about your own opinions
- Letting your ego get in the way (i.e., "it is my opinion so it must be right")
- Accepting the latest opinion you hear
- Reacting out of emotion rather than logic, reason, and common sense
- Avoiding the details of an issue (i.e., oversimplifying)
- Failing to consider motives
- Confusing opinions with facts
- Piggybacking on another person's opinion because you like them or are too lazy to research the topic in question

BEING STUBBORN, INFLEXIBLE, AND CLOSED-MINDED

Liars are often stubborn, inflexible, and closed-minded. They have made up their minds on an issue and nothing is going to change it. To convince you they are right, they will lie, distort, and deceive. Closed-minded people do not like to have their opinions challenged. They are often uncertain of their views and afraid they will not stand up to close scrutiny. Because of this, they are unable to defend their views in an open and honest debate.

It frustrates closed-minded people when others disagree. It frustrates them further when they cannot convince others their opinions are valid, and so they lie to make their views sound more palatable. They are more interested in being right than in discovering valid points of view from which they might learn and grow. Stubborn, inflexible, and closed-minded people follow their own plans and the stubbornness of their hearts.

President Joe Biden provided several telling examples of closed-minded stubbornness in 2023 when he was considering a run for re-election to the presidency. The first example was over the budget. At a time when the national debt of the United States was out of control and the government was debating raising the debt ceiling, President Biden presented a budget so loaded with new spending programs it would make American insolvent and turn the dollar into nothing but a useless piece of paper. When questioned about his budget proposal, the president dug in his heels and claimed it was not open to discussion. He refused to hear any concerns or recommendations, even from members of his own party.

On the issue of protecting Social Security and Medicare, the president also showed himself to be a closed-minded, inflexible, and stubborn liar. In his 2023 State of the Union Address, he claimed Republicans wanted to eliminate Social Security and Medicare. Republican representatives and senators attending the State of the Union Address were so outraged they broke with protocol and practically shouted the president down. They made it clear to all Americans on national television they would protect Social Security and Medicare. It was the president's proposed wasteful, unrealistic programs they would eliminate.

Even after Republicans pledged their support of Social Security and Medicare on national television, President Biden continued to claim in speeches and through his hapless press secretary they would eliminate these programs. This is the quintessential example of a closed-minded, inflexible, stubborn individual lying to advance his agenda.

Another example of stubborn closed-mindedness on the part of President Biden was his false claims about illegal immigrants crossing America's southern border. For the first three years of his presidency, Biden claimed the southern border was secure, while in reality, millions of immigrants crossed the border illegally, many of them hardened criminals, repeat offenders, and drug pushers. He repeatedly claimed the border was secure when everyone listening knew better, regardless their political persuasion. Much of the pushback the president received from his stubborn lies came from his own party.

Perhaps the president's most egregious example of closed-mindedness had to do with the issue of defunding the police. For his first two years in office, Biden supported Leftist mayors and city councils in big cities who advocated defunding the police. As they pulled the plug on their police departments, crime skyrocketed, so much so the Leftist ideologues who advocated defunding the police began to be kicked out of office in local elections.

Preparing to run for re-election, President Biden realized he and the left wing of the Democrat Party were in trouble on the issue of crime. So, what did he do? What every closed-minded, inflexible, and stubborn individual does in such situations. He lied. Biden began to claim against all evidence to the contrary—and there was lots of evidence—it was the Republicans who advocated defunding the police. His ego would not allow him to admit he and his Leftwing supporters were wrong when they eviscerated police departments around the country.

BEING TOO RECEPTIVE AND TOO WILLING TO ACCEPT ANY OPINION

Have you ever heard it said, "Some people will believe anything"? Unfortunately, it is true. We are lied to everyday by an ideologically driven mainstream media, purveyors of television ads, colleagues at work, fellow students, politicians, teachers, professors, and even friends. Yet some people willingly and meekly accept anything they hear from these sources. An individual once declared in an interview with a local reporter, "It must be true. I heard it on television." This individual, like anyone who accepts anything they hear, is naïve and gullible—two traits that will bring him nothing but grief throughout his life.

You have probably heard the adage by an unknown author, "Believe nothing you hear and half of what you see." This an exaggeration of course, but it makes a good point: never take input you receive at face value. Instead, weigh and examine what people tell you. There are a lot of lying media outlets, television ads, colleagues, fellow students, politicians, teachers, professors, and friends in the world.

People who are too receptive and too willing to accept any opinion often fall into the statistics trap. Knowing this, liars often misuse statistics to advance their agendas. Because they consist of numbers and data, some people confuse statistics with facts and truth. In reality, statistics can be used to prove anything no matter how false or misleading. They are easily twisted and distorted by bad actors trying to advance an agenda. Statistics are only as reliable as the data they are based on. You may have heard the maxim, "Garbage in—garbage out." If the data used to create statistics is not fair, accurate, and representative, the statistics are useless. You get garbage instead of facts. This explains why polls taken during political campaigns or public preference surveys are often misleading or downright wrong.

Statistics are supposed to be based on a representative sample of the population in question. If Democrats or Republicans include only members of their party in the polls they take, the result will be inaccurate statistics. Consider this example of how statistics can be misused. A city council member we will call Joann wanted to knock down a portion of an old area of town to make way for a major development project. Unbeknownst to her fellow council members and the mayor, the developer was a major contributor to her campaigns for office.

To convince her colleagues of the efficacy of her proposal, she decided to conduct a poll. The poll showed 90 percent of local citizens supported her proposal. Based on this poll, her fellow council members and the mayor gullibly voted to accept her proposal. It was only after demolition began and protestors lined the streets of the area in question when her naïve colleagues learned she skewed the results of the poll by surveying only people known to support the redevelopment project, including all the employees of the developer's company. Every member of the council and the mayor were voted out of office in the next election.

BEING ARROGANT AND OVERLY CONFIDENT OF YOUR OWN OPINIONS

Arrogance is a symptom of misguided pride. Arrogance causes people to look down on others as unworthy to challenge their opinions. A good definition of arrogance is a haughty spirit. It means an individual has an obnoxiously high but false sense of self-worth. Arrogant people behave as if they are superior as well as more important, worthy, and deserving than others. Interestingly, arrogance is rooted in insecurity.

Arrogant people are easy to recognize. They do not ask questions of others because they are interested only in their own views. Further, they are quick to attack anyone who differs with their views. If arrogant people had a collective motto, it would be "I know better than you because I am better than you." They attempt to improve their sense of self-worth by devaluing other people. It is as if knocking other people down builds them up. Interestingly, acting superior is often a defense for feelings of insecurity.

An example of an arrogant person who suffered because of his ego is a man we will call Mack. Mack was a high school football coach with a fair record at best, but one year his team went all the way to the state championship. Mack told anyone who would listen the success of the team was because of his superior coaching ability when, in fact, it was because some excellent players from out of state transferred to his school when their military parents were stationed at the local Air Force base.

Mack ran the team with an iron fist and brooked no complaints, suggestions, or recommendations from his coaching staff. His response when assistant coaches tried to suggest offensive or defensive strategies was to say, "I am the head coach, not you. If you knew better than me you would be the head coach." As result, turnover in his coaching staff was frequent.

When the state championship game rolled around, Mack—who did not like the passing game despite having an excellent passing quarterback and capable receivers—declared, "We are going to run the ball on them all night." When Mack's assistant coaches tried to tell him the opposing team had a defense that was able to stop the running game but was vulnerable to the passing game, Mack told them to do what they were told and leave game strategy to him.

No matter how many times his running backs were stopped for no gain, Mack kept pressing the running game. He simply could not admit to being wrong. As a result, his team lost the state championship by a lopsided margin. Predictably, Mack's coaching career went downhill from there and, after losing his head coaching job, Mack ended up selling used cars for a living.

LETTING EGO GET IN THE WAY

Arrogance and ego are closely related but not the same thing. Not everyone is arrogant, but everyone has an ego. It is an inborn personality trait while arrogance is an adopted trait. Ego is usually viewed as a negative, but this is not necessarily the case. Our self-esteem is a product of our ego. An ego balanced by humility can give an individual an appropriate sense of self-worth and self-confidence. But an out-of-control ego runs afoul of common sense, logic, reason, and experience.

Ego becomes a problem only when it swells up to the point it negatively controls our actions, decisions, and behavior. An

over-active ego creates an over-inflated sense of self-impor-
tance—a need to always be seen as smarter, better, and more
important than others. Egotists are conceited and self-absorbed.
Symptoms of an inflated ego are easy to spot. They include the
following:

- Inability to accept criticism even when it is constructive
- A need to feel smarter, better, and more important than others
- A need to always be right and always win
- Refusal to listen to others
- An entitlement mentality toward help received from others
- A propensity for taking credit and refusing blame
- A boundless need to be praised

Inability to accept criticism even when it is positive. Constructive
criticism can help us grow, learn, and improve, but to gain the
benefits of constructive criticism one must be willing to listen
to and accept it. People with an inflated ego refuse to accept
constructive criticism. Their ego will not allow them to admit
being wrong or even to having room for improvement no matter how reasonable and well-intended the feedback they get.

Need to feel smarter, better, and more important than others. The
worst nightmare for an individual with an inflated ego is to see
others excel, succeed, and earn meritorious recognition. Ego-
tism—the need to feel better, smarter, and more important than
others—is the opposite of humility. To egotists, a win for someone else is a loss for them. Egotists rarely, if ever, congratulate
other people on their success. Rather they tend to smolder with
jealousy. They cannot accept someone else being recognized for
meritorious performance. As a result, it is not uncommon for
an egotistical person to try to undermine the performance of
others at work, in the classroom, in the gym, or on the athletic field.

Need to always be right and always win. People who must always be right and always win do everything they can to glorify themselves. The need to always be right and always win is so powerful in egocentric people, they will do anything to satisfy it, including lying, cheating, and undermining others. In the classroom, they must make the highest grade. On the playing field, they must win the game. At work, they must get the best performance reviews and promotions. Anything less is unacceptable. On tests and the playing field, they will cheat to win. At work, they will lie to undermine the reputations of coworkers they see as competition. They will also take credit for work they did not do and deflect blame to others when their performance is subpar.

Refusal to listen to others. You may have heard the maxim, "You will learn more by listening than talking." This is good advice proven to be accurate many times. In spite of the value of listening to learn, improve, or gain a better understanding of another person's point of view, egocentric people feel no need to listen because in their minds they already know what is best. Further, they want to be the only person in the room.

Conversations with egotists are not conversations at all; they are one-way broadcasts of their opinions, recommendations, and beliefs. Those who try to have a conversation with an egocentric person find themselves constantly interrupted, a behavior that says, "I don't want to hear it." Egocentric people know listening to others might cause them to question their foregone conclusions and self-serving opinions; something they cannot accept.

Entitlement mentality toward help received from others. People who receive help from others are usually grateful. They show their gratitude by thanking the giver. Not so with egotists. Egocentric people have an entitlement mentality toward the help received from others. They think they are entitled to it, so why be thankful. Further, egotists are unable to admit to themselves or others that they need help, thus they do not appreciate the help they receive. In fact, some resent it.

Taking credit and refusing blame. Most work is done in teams. Most athletic sports are team sports. Even in school and college, students are often given group assignments. Teamwork does not sit well with people who seek credit and avoid blame. Egotists want to be the star of the show; they seek attention and recognition whether they deserve it or not. Further, in a team setting they insist the team do things their way even if it is not the best way. When their way fails, egocentric people are quick to blame the other members of the team. To do otherwise is to admit, in spite of their inflated egos, they are not perfect and can be wrong. Doing so is anathema to them.

Need to be praised. To an egocentric person, praise is like milk to a baby; they must have it. The ego of this kind of individual is a fragile part of their personality always in need of maintenance. That maintenance comes in the form of praise and recognition. Humble believers know praise is a dangerous concept that can create a negative and unhelpful need in people. No matter what you achieve in human terms, humility will be an asset.

A woman we will call Jennifer provides a good example of what can happen to people who need to feel smarter, better, and more important than others. Jennifer exhibited all the characteristics explained herein. Her need to feel better, smarter, and more important began to show itself in middle school. She was a member of her school's chorus. When tryouts for soloist were announced, Jennifer set her mind on winning the competition.

Unwilling to let her singing do the talking for her, Jennifer began telling anyone who would listen that her voice was better than the other contestants. She even tried to recruit members of the chorus to support her and recommend her to the music teacher who would judge the competition. When she did not win, Jennifer quit the chorus in a huff.

In high school Jennifer set her mind on being selected "Outstanding Student of the Year." The winner would be determined by grade point average (GPA). Jennifer had a good GPA, but so did a classmate. He was her competition for the award. The selection would come down to which of them scored highest on a comprehensive end-of-year exam all seniors had to take.

Unwilling to leave the competition to merit, Jennifer decided to cheat. The boy she was competing against prepared a comprehensive set of study notes—something that took not just hours but days to prepare. When one day he left his books on his desk after class, Jennifer took his study notes. Rather than study the notes, she took them into the exam and tried to use them to cheat on the test. Caught in the act, Jennifer was given a failing grade on the exam and suspended from school for a week.

In college Jennifer continued her dishonest ways to make herself feel better, smarter, and more important than others. Rather than write the essays she was assigned, she downloaded them off the internet. Whenever she could, Jennifer cheated on tests. If other students questioned her input in class discussions, Jennifer belittled them and their opinions. Once, when most of her classmates disagreed with her, she stomped out of class in a fit of anger.

After college, Jennifer began a career in real estate. True to form, she was determined to be selected "Sales Representative of the Year" in her first year on the job. Unable to keep up with her more experienced colleagues, Jennifer began to poach their clients. She also criticized them when talking to potential clients saying things such as "You don't want to work with John. He won't return your calls and won't follow up on your requests. Let me help you. I guarantee you will be satisfied."

It did not take long for her colleagues to figure out what Jennifer was doing and bring their complaints to the boss.

After looking into the situation, the owner of the real estate firm gave Jennifer the option of resigning or being fired. She resigned but not before telling the boss and her colleague they were a bunch of "losers." Jennifer's need to feel better, smarter, and more important than others led to nothing but grief throughout her life.

SUMMARY

- Behaviors that critical thinkers must avoid include being closed-minded, inflexible, and stubborn; being too receptive and too willing to accept any opinion; being arrogant and overly confident about your own opinions; letting your ego get in the way; accepting the latest opinion you hear; reacting to input you receive out of emotion rather than logic, reason, experience, and common sense; avoiding details; failing to consider motives; confusing opinions with facts; and piggybacking onto another person's opinion without giving it due consideration.
- Egotistical people are arrogant and self-absorbed. Symptoms of an inflated ego are easy to spot and include the following: inability to accept criticism even when it is constructive; need to feed smarter, better, and more important than others; need to always be right and always win; refusal to listen to others; an entitlement mentality toward help received from others; a propensity for taking undue credit and refusing to accept due blame; and a boundless need to be praised.

3

RECOGNIZE BIAS IN THE MESSAGE

*D*ifferent sources refer to bias in different terms, including partiality, favoritism, and snobbery. Bias, regardless what it's called, means favoring without reason one side of an argument, issue, or question. Biased messages are heavily weighted to one side. They are also overly opinionated. They rely on unsubstantiated claims, carefully selected, seemingly logical, but incomplete information, and sometimes downright lies. Biased messengers leave out important information or alter the facts to support their opinion or agenda in an attempt to convince others to agree with them, make a desired decision, or take certain action.

As we show in our book *American Gulags: Marxist Tyranny in Higher Education*, one of the most prevalent examples of biased messengers may be found in our nation's colleges and universities. Radicals from the 1960s and '70s became professors and took over the institutions of higher education. They did then, and still do, espouse a Marxist doctrine that attacks all of America's supposed ills while leaving out what is good, right, and meritorious about our country.

These Marxist professors are elitists who exhibit intellectual snobbery in biasing their teaching and the requirements for passing their classes. Students who try to push back against the bias often are publicly belittled, fail their courses, and are refused admission to graduate school. What is happening in our nation's colleges and universities is an egregious manifestation of bias.

You will also find bias in churches. You may have encountered a self-righteous type in church who criticizes other church members for their supposed shortcomings instead of fellowshipping with and mentoring them. They believe they are morally better than other believers. These biased individuals present themselves to the congregation as holier than all and yet leave out important teachings from the Bible.

Bias is present in all fields of endeavor. A specific example is the refusal of NFL coaches to even consider drafting quarterback Charlie Ward out of college. As quarterback of the Florida State Seminoles, Ward won the Heisman Trophy and a national championship. He could pass, run, and mastermind the offense for the Seminoles. By all appearances he would be selected in the first round of the NFL draft, but to the surprise of many he was not even considered. Why? Size bias. NFL scouts ignoring his obvious talent, left out his achievements at Florida State, and claimed he was too small to play in the NFL. A number of quarterbacks his size have excelled in the NFL.

TYPES OF BIAS TO RECOGNIZE AND REJECT

It is important for you to understand bias when you are discussing, hearing, or reading a message. If you know how to look for bias in the message, you will be better equipped to rebut or even refute the message. By recognizing bias and rejecting it, you can prevent yourself from being lured into accepting a false message and unwisely acting on it. There are several different types of bias you need to learn to look for. The most prominent of them are as follows:

- Confirmation bias
- Cultural bias
- In-group bias
- Oversimplification bias
- Information bias
- Recall bias

CONFIRMATION BIAS

People who are guilty of confirmation bias look for information that supports their preconceived notions and ignore any information that does not. This is the most common form of bias liars and distorters employ. This type of bias is sometimes called the "ostrich effect" because of the belief ostriches bury their heads in the sand to avoid seeing things they do not want to see. Or is it they *think* they can't be seen?

An example of confirmation bias occurs when politicians who are pushing an agenda tell the public only the favorable aspects of their proposed policies but carefully leave out the negatives. For example, when politicians propose "forgiving" student debt for college students. They claim it will enhance the economy by allowing the students to spend the money that otherwise would have gone to servicing their debt. What they do not say is expecting taxpayers who never had the chance to go to college to pay the debts of students who make unwise decisions about loans is patently unfair. They do not speak to reinforcing irresponsibility in college students who will expect the government to rescue them when they overspend on credit cards or purchase a home or car they cannot afford. Finally, they say nothing about the cost and how much their proposal will inflate the national debt.

CULTURAL BIAS

Cultural bias occurs when an individual thinks people from other cultures are inferior. It creates stereotypes that cause the biased to discount others in discussions and debates. Consider the following example of cultural bias. Your employer has an opening and has advertised to fill it. The best qualified candidate is Hispanic. One of the members of the interview team opposes hiring the Hispanic candidate because of cultural bias. He tells the other members of the team, "We don't want to hire this guy. Hispanics are lazy." This individual simply ignores the Hispanic candidate's education, experience, and proven track record. To him, cultural bias trumps qualifications.

IN-GROUP BIAS

This type of bias is similar to cultural bias in that it causes people to favor others who are like them, except the group they identify with is smaller. Their attitude toward people from outside the group is "she's not one of us." Martha was the victim of in-group bias when she was in college. She pledged an elite sorority, of which she easily exceeded the stated qualifications. But Martha was blackballed by several members of the sorority because she went to a public high school instead of an elite private school and her background was middle-class rather than wealthy. In short, Martha was not part of the in-group—not "one of them."

In-group bias is a form of snobbery that causes people to advance their causes and agendas on the basis of incomplete and irrelevant information. For example, sometimes in-group bias is used to influence decisions about hiring employees. Rather than claim she is not one of us, people who practice in-group bias will argue "she's not a good fit." A lot of employers have missed out on hiring talented, dynamic people who could make a difference because they allowed themselves to be hoodwinked by in-group bias.

OVERSIMPLIFICATION BIAS

People who indulge in oversimplification bias do not wish to invest the time and effort necessary to examine all aspects of an issue. As a result, they oversimplify. Worse yet, they tend to think they are smarter than others who do not see things as they do. People who oversimplify think they are better able to get to the heart of a problem than others who get bogged down in the weeds with details. You can recognize oversimplification bias when someone says, "This issue isn't complicated at all. The obvious solution is . . ." but you see relevant details that have not been considered.

An example of oversimplification bias occurred over and over when Russia first invaded Ukraine. The United States wanted to respond by placing sanctions on Russia. Numerous people, guilty of oversimplification bias, claimed the answer is simple. The European nations should immediately stop buying Russian oil and gas. This, they argued, would cripple Russia's economy. But they did not consider such factors as where European nations would get the oil and gas they need so badly. Nor did they consider what would happen if Russia found other countries to buy its oil—countries such as China. Shutting off Russian oil and gas to Europe was a good idea, but it wasn't as simple an issue as some people argued.

INFORMATION BIAS

People who engage in information bias try to bury their opponents in data, most of which is irrelevant and most of which, if not all, they have not read themselves. The idea is to impress opponents with stacks of data which make them think the biased person is better prepared than they are and, as a result, more likely to be right. In reality, people who engage in information bias wind up arguing from ignorance because they do not know what information is contained in the reports and articles they stack up.

Mary Lou was subjected to information bias during a discussion at work. The team was discussing a new direction for marketing its products that would incorporate greater use of the internet and social media. The head of marketing, knowing Mary Lou would make her recommendation, brought stacks of profit/loss statements, annual reports, and articles from marketing journals—information he never read. In response to Mary Lou's recommendation he claimed, "I think we should just keep doing what we have always done. I've never seen a better way."

Mary Lou, a critical thinker and better prepared than the head of marketing, responded, "Just because you've never seen a better way doesn't mean there isn't one." Then she picked up one of the marketing journals he brought in but not read, turned to a specific article titled "Ten Reasons to Market Your Products on the Internet" and read the article's conclusion. Mary Lou's recommendation was approved.

RECALL BIAS

People who engage in recall bias try to press their opinions by relying on information everyone in the discussion can easily recall. It is an enticing strategy because we all tend to favor information familiar to us, information comfortable to us. The problem with this strategy is information we can easily recall is not always complete or even accurate. There may be additional information pertaining to the issue that is relevant and important.

A husband and wife were discussing a trip to Disneyworld but were tight on money. They were trying to decide if they could afford it. The husband, who really wants to make the trip claimed, "We both remember what the tickets, rooms, and meals cost us last time we went to Disneyworld." His wife countered, "That was three years ago. Prices have probably gone up since then." By making a few phone calls and doing some online research, the wife was able to show her husband the information he recalled was no longer accurate.

Victoria Rodriguez had a forty-year career as a civil engineer, in part because she was a skilled critical thinker. Over the course of her career, she had to recognize, confront, and reject every kind of bias explained herein. Early in her career Victoria faced several instances of cultural bias, not because of her Hispanic heritage but because she was a woman in a profession dominated by men. However, slowly but surely her male colleagues began to recognize her talent and welcomed her on their projects. In fact, they began to seek her out and invite her to join their teams.

Once she was established in the eyes of her male colleagues, the kind of bias Victoria had to deal with most often was confirmation bias. An example of this type of bias occurred on a project in which the job was to design and build a high school football stadium. Victoria's company specialized in prestressed concrete and would provide the seats. The concrete seats would be supported by a steel understructure provided by another company.

This was the first project the team leader had been responsible for and he was determined to bring it in on time and within budget. When he presented his plan and schedule to the project team, the steel specifications were conspicuously missing. When Victoria asked about them, the team leader responded, "I've looked the steel specifications over and they are fine. Let's move on." Victoria objected saying, "It would be better if everyone on the team examined the specifications. The more eyes on them the better."

Because of Victoria's critical thinking, the team leader was compelled to share the steel specifications with his team

members. Victoria and several other team members saw immediately the steel company specified a lower grade of steel than
was called for. It turned out the team leader knew of the problem but did not raise the issue for fear of slowing down the
project and increasing the final cost of it. The rationale side of
the argument, raised by Victoria, was the steel the company
planned to use might fail and the stadium seats collapse. The
steel company was compelled to alter its specifications and use
the proper grade of steel.

SUMMARY

- Bias is favoring, without reason, one side of an argument,
  issue, or question. Biased information is heavily weighted
  to one side. It is also overly opinionated. It relies on unsubstantiated claims, carefully selected but incomplete or inaccurate information, and, sometimes, downright lies.
- The most prominent kinds of bias to recognize and reject
  include confirmation bias, cultural bias, in-group bias, oversimplification bias, information bias, and recall bias.

4

EVALUATE THE MOTIVES
OF PEOPLE

*O*ne of the most important skills you can learn as a critical
thinker is to evaluate the motives of people who give you
advice, information, or recommendations. Motives are the
driving force behind the actions we take and the decisions we
make. They are why we do what we do, which amounts to
satisfying our perceived personal needs. Motives are a natural
part of the human condition; we all have them and they can be
good or bad.

MASLOW'S HIERARCHY OF NEEDS

The acknowledged leader in studies of human motivation is an
American psychologist named Abraham Maslow. Maslow
developed a model of human needs called the Hierarchy of
Needs which begins with lowest human needs and proceeds to
the highest. Here are the categories of needs all people have
according to Maslow:

1. Safety and security
2. Freedom from fear plus routine

3. Connectedness, being part of a group
4. Achievement, status, and self-esteem
5. Self-fulfillment, confidence

To apply Maslow's model, it is necessary to first understand the individual needs and how they apply in the context of this book. Human needs are motives.

SAFETY AND SECURITY MOTIVE

We all want to be safe and secure. This is why people install security systems in their homes and lock their doors at night. Safety and security are powerful needs that can shape how people live and respond to others. Mothers tell their children, "Don't talk to strangers." Automobiles have seat belts and air bags. Public schools have police officers on site as guards. Parents keep a close eye on their children at playgrounds. Citizens avoid certain areas in their towns and tell their teenagers to be home before dark.

The power of the needs for safety and security proved itself in 2023 when cities run by Leftwing ideologues defunded their police departments only to see crime skyrocket. There were riots, looting, arson, smash-and-grab burglaries, and attacks on storekeepers and civilians. Worse yet, the murder rate and violence in general in these big cities went through the ceiling. Citizens, regardless their political persuasions, demanded the mayors and city council members of their cities rehire the police and get crime under control. Many of the elected officials who refused were quickly turned out of office. What Leftwing ideologues learned is the need for safety and security trumps ideology.

It is important to understand the need for safety and security encompasses more than feeling safe in your homes or out in public. People with an agenda often fear for their job security, status, and other factors. This sense of fear can make them lie, distort, and deceive to protect these things. Their agenda is not the best decision but their own perceived personal needs outweigh everything else.

A city council member we will call Larry tried to convince his fellow members not to fund the police in spite of the crime that had overtaken their city. Larry was a social worker by profession and wanted to increase funding for social services by diverting funds from the police department. He promised his colleagues in social services the increased funding, his status with his colleagues—a powerful need for Larry—would be diminished if he did not come through with the promised funding. When you consider motives relating to safety and security, make sure you look beyond the physical needs of people.

FREEDOM FROM FEAR MOTIVE

Fear is a powerful motivator second only to safety and security. In fact, Maslow could have combined the two. Most of the things we do to ensure our safety and security are based on fear. We fear someone might break into our home and harm our family so we install security systems. We fear we might be assaulted while in public so we choose where we go and when carefully. We fear for our job security so we work hard to impress the boss or we join unions.

You might have heard someone say, "All I fear is death and taxes." If that is true, the individual making the claim is an exception to the rule. The most common fears of adult Americans include the following: safety and security, public speaking, heights, going to the dentist, snakes, flying, spiders and other insects, mice, dogs, thunder and lightning, rejection, loss of job security, failure, and sickness. Fear can cause people to do or say things they might not otherwise do or say. Consider the following examples of how some people react to fear.

- Terrence was deathly afraid of flying. When his boss asked him to fly from Atlanta to New York to finalize an important deal for the company, rather than simply admit the truth, Terrance claimed his wife was seriously ill and he needed to stay close by to tend to her.
- Debbie was afraid of public speaking. When she was asked to represent her company at a charity event and give the keynote speech, she waited until the day of the event and called in sick.
- Geena was afraid of failure. Consequently, in college classes she cheated to make sure she would pass.
- Marvin was afraid of losing his job security. He responded by taking credit for the work of his colleagues.

CONNECTEDNESS—BEING PART OF A GROUP MOTIVE

Most people are social beings by nature. They like being part of groups. Social beings derive a sense of belonging, companionship, and support from being a member of a group. The groups people voluntarily join are comprised of members who share the same interests, concerns, experiences, and values. This is where the sense of belonging, companionship, and support come from.

There are numerous kinds of groups such as the Elks, Veterans of Foreign Wars (VFW), Boy Scouts, Girl Scouts, PTOs, athletic teams, work teams, chambers of commerce, student government associations in high school and college, and thousands of fan clubs for sports teams and entertainers. Of course, the ultimate group is your own family. How many groups in your community can you name?

Most of the groups you can name have a positive mission and worthy goals. Generally speaking, they exist to do good work. For example, parents join PTOs to improve the quality of instruction their children receive. However, not all groups have positive, helpful missions or goals. For example, Antifa and the Ku Klux Klan have large memberships but their missions and goals are hardly worthy. In fact, just the opposite.

One of the benefits of being in a group is they promote critical thinking because its members admire fellow members whose rational analysis helps achieve the goals of the group. Another way groups promote critical thinking is the issue of leadership. All groups must have a leader. Folks who are able to think through issues tend to stand out in the eyes of their associates in a positive way and, as a result, become leaders in groups.

SELF-ACTUALIZATION MOTIVE

Self-actualization is a powerful motive—a need most people strive to satisfy. Self-actualized people are perfectly happy, perfectly satisfied, and perfectly content. They have realized their full potential as human beings and become all they are capable of being. As you might imagine, achieving self-actualization is a tall order. Self-actualization is a need few people ever truly satisfy. But there is good news. Critical thinkers are more likely to achieve self-actualization than those whose lives are focused on self-centered considerations such as what they think, feel, and want.

Achieving a state of self-actualization does not mean people never have problems. Quite the contrary. Self-actualized people still face difficulties in life. Nothing can shield human beings from experiencing the challenges of living in an imperfect world. This fact is one more reason why critical thinkers are more likely to achieve self-actualization. They recognize their limits and know how to apply their unique talents, insights, and strengths to mitigating the problems they face. They approach life in a way that takes full advantage of their strengths and mitigates their weaknesses. They do not complicate their lives by making use of deception, distortion, and lying. Critical thinkers know, regardless individual thoughts, feelings, and desires, the truth always leads to a better place than lying.

Characteristics associated with self-actualized people include: dedication to the truth; an ability to avoid being improperly influenced by the opinions of others; willingness to deal with ambiguity and uncertainty; tolerance of those whose worldview differs from theirs without being swayed by the differences; realization that a lot of things in life are bigger than they are; strong sense of fairness and justice; personal responsibility; and, finally, an expectation of being held accountable for their decisions and subsequent actions.

Considering the motives of those you interact with is an essential part of critical thinking. Critical thinking will improve your life, your decisions, your actions, and your reputation among peers and colleagues. Those who think objectively are more likely to achieve self-actualization. Those who fail to think objectively will live lives mired in problems of their own making by forever seeking to satisfy needs based on "I think," "I need," and "I want."

SUMMARY

- One of the most important skills you can learn as someone who wants to be a critical thinker is to evaluate the motives of people who give you advice, information, or recommendations. Motives are the driving force behind the decisions people make and actions they take. Motives are aimed at satisfying our perceived needs. They are part of the human condition; we all have motives. Motives can be good or bad. The motives behind the recommendations of people who apply the "I think, I feel, and I want" model are often bad.
- Abraham Maslow, an American psychologist, developed a Hierarchy of Needs that explain the motives of people, good and bad. Those needs from the most basic to the highest are as follows: safety and security; freedom from fear; connectedness—being part of a group; achievement, status, and self-esteem; and self-fulfillment and confidence.

- An example of the need for safety and security can be seen in people who install high-tech security systems in their homes.
- An example of freedom from fear can be seen in people who avoid heights, flying, public speaking, going to the doctor or dentist, snakes, spiders, mice, dogs, thunder and lightning, rejection, loss of job security, failure, and sickness.
- An example of the need for connectedness can be seen in people who join groups of like-minded people including such organizations as the PTO, Elks, Veterans of Foreign Wars (VFW), chambers of commerce, and fan clubs.
- Self-actualized people are perfectly happy, satisfied, and content. A lot of people spend their lives trying to satisfy this, the highest of Maslow's needs.

5

DISTINGUISH BETWEEN EXPLANATIONS AND RATIONALIZATIONS

*R*ationalizing is a favorite tactic of people who base their opinions on the "I think, I feel, or I want" model. Rationalizing is a defense mechanism in which people try to justify difficult, inaccurate, or unacceptable assertions by presenting seemingly logical, plausible reasons. Rationalizing makes its practitioners feel better about themselves because it allows them to believe their own excuses and lies rather than admit they are wrong. Rationalizing is not reasoning as some like to claim. Reasoning begins with verified facts and drawing appropriate conclusions from those facts. Rationalizing begins with a conclusion and tries to justify it using seemingly logical assertions.

Rationalizing is also not intellectualizing. Intellectualizing involves detaching oneself from feelings and focusing on verifiable facts. Intellectualism leads people to follow the facts wherever they might lead and to accept the facts no matter how difficult that might be. Rationalizing, on the other hand, involves making excuses to conceal facts, motives, and research findings. People rationalize because it makes them feel better about themselves.

Explaining, on the other hand, involves presenting information to clarify a position and make it understandable. An example of rationalizing is a high school student who is denied membership in a campus club. He might rationalize the rejection by claiming, "It's a crummy club. I didn't really want to join it anyway." Critical thinkers must learn to distinguish between explanations and rationalizations because there are dangers in accepting rationalizations. They lead to bad decisions, inaccurate conclusions, and errant assumptions.

TYPES OF RATIONALIZATIONS

There are four types of rationalizations you should be familiar with. They are practical, theoretical, substantive, and formal. Let's look at these four types of rationalizations so you can apply this knowledge when dealing with individuals who base their opinions on "I think," "I feel," and "I want."

1. *Practical rationalization* involves beginning with the conclusion you want and then looking for arguments supporting that conclusion. For example, politicians with a certain agenda might decide allowing unfettered access to our southern border is a good idea. To justify this conclusion, they look for arguments such as humanitarianism and helping people begin better lives while ignoring all the downside arguments against open access.

2. *Theoretical rationalization* involves using hypothetical, abstract information in an attempt to alter reality. For example, an individual might hypothesize that pain is a good thing to validate his position on a certain medical procedure.

3. *Substantive rationalization* involves basing an opinion on whether or not the proposed action is likely to have a desirable outcome. For example, the person making the proposal might judge something to be good because it accords with his values. But what are those values? Will the outcome be positive in reality or just positive for the person making the proposal?

4. *Formal rationalization* involves deciding what is most important to the person making an assertion or proposal and using logic and deduction to support their position. For example, a developer might want to knock down several older buildings and build condominiums. To her, the most important part of the proposal is knocking down a certain building. Consequently, she focuses her arguments on the supposed benefits of replacing that specific building which is an eyesore and a crime magnet.

We mentioned earlier that rationalization is a dangerous concept because it can lead to poor decisions and unhelpful actions. In addition to being dangerous, rationalizing has a distinct disadvantage when compared to critical thinking, logical explanations, and valid reasoning. The disadvantage is rationalization uses human capital without resulting in adequate returns. When people invest their time, energy, and minds in making excuses for invalid assertions or proposals, they are wasting a valuable resource: human capital. Investing human capital should result in positive returns. Human capital includes brain power, creativity, talent, intelligence, and energy. Wasting these things on trying to defend the indefensible is like wasting monetary capital but worse.

DEFENSES USED BY RATIONALIZERS

Rationalizers know they are trying to justify the unjustifiable, but their propensity for applying the "I think, I need, and I want" model is too strong for them to overcome. As a result, they have developed a number of defenses for rationalizing. These defenses include denial, displacement, repression, sublimation, projection, and reaction formation. People who operate strictly according to what they think, feel, or want use these defenses to make themselves feel better when their rationalizations do not have the desired effect. As a critical thinker, you need to be able to recognize these defenses:

- *Denial defense.* When things do not go their way, people who rationalize their assertions and recommendations are faced with an ego problem: failure. To feel better about themselves, they may deny the unwanted event or decision ever happened. An example of the denial defense is when a husband has argued he is fine but his wife thinks he has health problems. A few tests at the emergency room shows the wife is right. Unable to face being proven wrong and the seriousness of his affliction, he simply denies anything is wrong.

- *Displacement defense.* When things do not work out for individuals who apply the "I think, I feel, and I want" model, they sometimes respond by displacing their anger or frustration. For example, when a project at work fails, the team leader for the project might take his frustration out on other team members or unleash his anger on his spouse or children. Displacement is used to blame others for one's own failures.

- *Repression defense.* This defense involves blocking out unwanted information by refusing to think about it, talk about it, or even admit it exists. An example of the repression defense is when an individual is involved in a serious automobile accident in which a child is killed. The accident is the driver's fault. Rather than deal with the unpleasant memory, she represses it and refuses to acknowledge its existence.

- *Sublimation defense.* Sublimation involves converting bad impulses into positive action. For example, rather than becoming angry and beating on the screen of a malfunctioning ATM in the middle of your transaction, you decide to drive around the block and cool down. Then you go inside the bank and straighten out the problem. Sublimation is a positive form of defense that is more likely to be used by critical thinkers than rationalizers.
- *Projection defense.* This form of defense involves mentally transferring (projecting) unacceptable thoughts or feelings to someone else. If individuals become angry because their rationalizations are not working, they might transfer their anger to someone else. This makes them feel more noble. For example, a husband becomes angry because his wife does not want to eat out at a restaurant. Rather than admit his anger and deal with it, the husband projects it onto his wife. He might say, "What are you getting angry about; it's just a suggestion?"
- *Reaction formation defense.* This form of defense involves substituting a negative impulse with its opposite. A common example of this defense is when someone is sad or angry but claims to be happy.

RECOGNIZING WHEN SOMEONE IS RATIONALIZING

It is not difficult to recognize when someone is rationalizing instead of explaining. Four sure signs of rationalizing are blaming, minimizing, deflecting, and attacking. When things do not go well for a rationalizer, she might respond by blaming others for her failure. This is the blaming response. Minimizing is when people downplay the rejection of their ideas or proposals as if it does not matter to them. A typical minimizing response is, "It's no big deal." Deflecting involves claiming the issue raised against their assertions is not the real issue. Finally, attacking is putting into action the belief that a strong offense is the best defense. If people do not accept your proposals or opinions, attack them.

Alma noticed whenever her colleague, Angus, made a presentation at work, he had a habit of getting angry and projecting his anger onto others if they did not accept his proposals. He also tended to blame others for his own failures and shortcomings. Alma liked Angus and thought he had potential, so she decided to talk with him about his habit of rationalizing.

"Angus, I would like to discuss your tendency to rationalize rather than explain when making proposals. I think you have enormous potential, but I am afraid rationalizing rather than seeking and presenting the truth is going to hold you back." Angus's first response was to use the denial defense popular with people who apply the "I think, I need, and I want" model. "I don't get angry and I don't project my anger on others. You're the one who is angry." This denial was said in a huff. Angus got angry with Alma for calling him out about rationalizing rather than explaining.

When Alma responded, "Angus, listen to yourself. You are angry now and are projecting your anger onto me. This tendency is going to hurt your career. I'm not the only one of your colleagues who has noticed your propensity for rationalizing." This statement gave Angus pause. Above all things, he wanted to succeed in his career. Angus was very ambitious and determined to climb the career ladder in his current job. He decided right then to make a change.

SUMMARY

- Rationalizing is a favorite tactic of those who base their opinions on the "I think, I feel, and I want" model. Rationalizing is a defense mechanism employed by people to justify difficult, inaccurate, or unacceptable feelings by presenting logical, plausible, reasonable attempts at explaining. Of course, rationalizing and explaining are polar opposite concepts.

- There are several types of rationalizations including the following: practical rationalization, theoretical rationalization, substantive rationalization, and formal rationalization.
- Defenses used by those who rationalize include the following: denial defense, displacement defense, repression defense, sublimation defense, projection defense, and reaction formation defense.

6

DO YOUR HOMEWORK—
RESEARCH THE FACTS

*T*here will be times when even the most skilled critical thinker cannot sort through the distortion, deception, and lies they are subjected to. When this happens, research is the answer. Research is a tool critical thinkers must have in their toolbox. It allows them to add to their knowledge, understand issues, reject lies, and support truth. However, research will serve its purpose only if it is good research. Haphazard research is the enemy of critical thinking.

The guiding principles of good research are honesty, transparency, and independence. In order to ensure good research, researchers must be honest with themselves. They must dig into the issue in question as deeply as possible and go where the facts take them. Just selectively searching out a few incomplete facts supporting the researcher's point of view will negate the value of the research.

An example of honest research is an individual at work who is proposing a new product he thinks will help the company in the marketplace. When several of his colleagues challenge his proposal, he asks for time to research his ideas. The deeper he gets into his research, the more obvious it becomes there are problems with his proposed new product. As an honest researcher, he lets his colleagues know about his findings and drops the idea for a new product.

Transparency in research is important. It means ensuring research methods, analysis, and interpretative choices are open and visible to others who will want to evaluate them. An example of transparent research is when a college student thoroughly describes the research methods she used on her graduate thesis so others can easily replicate the research and analyze the findings. In this way, they can determine if their findings match those of the graduate student.

Another example is when a business colleague says, "I Googled the idea. Here are the sites I visited." This would allow his colleagues to go to those sites to determine if they interpret the data in the same way as the researcher. It would also allow them to determine if there are informative sites the original researcher overlooked. The ability to visit the same sites as the original researcher and to look for other relevant sites makes the research transparent.

Independent research occurs when researchers are free of, or able to resist outside influences and pressure that might alter their choices or interpretations. Independence is important in research because it promotes critical thinking and accurate results. An example of independent research occurs when a junior member of a firm is able to resist pressure from his boss to skew the results of his research to support her superior's point of view. An example of research that is not independent occurs when the researcher believes the data will undercut a project important to a good friend and colleague and, therefore, skews the data.

HOW TO CONDUCT RESEARCH

Critical thinkers do not have to be accomplished research scientists who spend every workday of their lives conducting research in fully equipped, technologically advanced laboratories. Rather, any critical thinker can conduct good research. The reason for this is accomplished research scientists not only conduct research, they write articles for professional journals containing the findings of their research.

Thus, your first method for conducting research should be to identify relevant articles in professional journals. Fortunately, you can do this without spending hours in libraries as was the case in the bad old days of research when unscrupulous researchers conducted what came to be known as *razor blade research*. They would locate the professional journal they wanted—not always an easy task—turn to the article in question and cut it out of the journal. This phenomenon persisted in those ancient days before copy machines were readily available in libraries.

Rather than spend time in libraries, you can use the second method of research for critical thinkers: the internet. These days most articles found in professional journals can also be found online. The key is to recognize which articles are valid, dependable sources and which are not. This is fairly easy to do. Once you identify promising information on the internet, look at its source. If the source is a reputable organization such as the American Medical Association (AMA) or the American Society for Quality (ASQ), you can probably depend on the article's validity. What you want to watch for is information that is really an advertisement rather than a valid article or just the scribblings of non-expert authors with an agenda.

The final research method for critical thinkers is asking acknowledged experts on the topic in question for advice. Even though these individuals are experts in their fields, it is important to be aware of bias in the advice they give. Even the most informed, talented experts can be guilty of bias.

BENEFITS OF CONDUCTING GOOD RESEARCH

Good research offers at least two important benefits. The first benefit is it adds to or clarifies the data relevant to a given issue or assertion. It is not uncommon for right-minded people—people who seek the truth—to disagree about an issue they are discussing. When this happens, good research can help them distinguish between fact and fiction. This, in turn, will allow them to make decisions and act on the basis of accurate data and clear interpretations.

An example of an organization that enjoyed the benefits of good research after a question was raised during a team meeting sets the stage for research into an issue. The water treatment team for a large city is trying to decide if the city's water is sufficiently affected by a chemical spill to shut down tap water and require people to drink only bottled water. Doing so will raise the hackles of citizens, particularly of restaurant owners who depend on a ready supply of tap water. Consequently, it is important to nail down a defensible answer. If the team errs in one direction, it will be criticized for overreacting. If it errs in the other direction, it will be attacked for putting citizens in danger.

After researching the contaminant in question, the team finds the chemical is not just toxic to human beings, but dangerously so. As a result, they decide to shut down the city's tap water. The decision is picked apart by media mavens who know nothing about the chemical and would not understand the findings of the team's research even if they bothered to examine it. This, in turn, raised protests from restaurant owners and others with a stake in the decision. However, the protests quickly died down when the team was able to show several deaths occurred in other locations when the deadly chemical got into the water supply.

The example of a city's water supply being contaminated demonstrates the importance of good research by critical thinkers. The research in this case provided critical guidance to the city's water treatment team allowing it to make the right decision in a difficult, seemingly no-win situation. It also added to their body of knowledge which, in turn, made the team better prepared to handle similar situations in the future and to assist other cities facing the same situation.

VALUE OF GOOD RESEARCH

Good research has value beyond its practical benefits as demonstrated in the previous section. Those benefits include the following:

- Promotes truth seeking
- Adds to the body of knowledge generally and specifically
- Allows stakeholders to learn in ways that improve their decisions and subsequent actions
- Helps in achieving better understanding of issues, problems, and questions
- Develops a valuable skill for critical thinkers
- Ensures important decisions are based on up-to-date information

As an aspiring critical thinker, you need to know the value of good research. Let's look at those benefits.

- ***Promotes truth seeking.*** Truth seeking is important because it frees us from ignorance, inaccuracies, false perceptions, and error, all of which lead to bad decisions and unhelpful actions. Critical thinkers do not seek validation of their preconceived notions; they seek the truth. Seeking the truth frees us from ignorance and error while also promoting honesty and integrity.
- ***Adds to the body of knowledge generally and specifically.*** With every issue or topic there is a general body of knowledge and a specific body of knowledge. The general body of knowledge includes broad facts about the issue in

question. The specific body of knowledge surrounding an issue pertains to just those facts relating to the issue in question and no other topic. Research increases our knowledge of both. Both are important to critical thinkers because both help in revealing the truth about the issue in question.

- *Allows researchers to learn in ways that improve decisions and actions.* Research clears away the ambiguity surrounding debatable issues. In doing so, researchers learn about the issue in question in ways that help them improve decisions and actions taken as a result of their decisions.

- *Helps in achieving a better understanding of issues, problems, and questions.* The better and more thorough one's understanding of an issue, problem, or question the better decisions will be when based on that understanding. This, of course, assumes honesty and integrity in conducting research. This is the bad news. The good news is critical thinkers who can demonstrate a better understanding of the issue in question are more likely to influence other stakeholders who may be on the fence or may initially oppose a given point of view.

- *Develops valuable skills for critical thinkers.* Research skills are critically important to critical thinkers; they are fundamental to how critical thinkers approach a debatable issue. When you know how to conduct research, whether on the internet or in libraries, you have a powerful advantage over the "I think, I feel, and I want" crowd.

- *Ensures decisions are made on the basis of up-to-date information.* Good research is based on the latest information available on a topic. Basing decisions on outdated information is as big a mistake as succumbing to the "I think, I feel, and I want" model. When you conduct research online, read professional journals, or listen to an expert on the issue in question, make sure the information you accept is up-to-date. Be especially attentive to dated or biased information when researching on the internet.

CONDUCTING FORMAL RESEARCH

As a critical thinker, the kind of research you may be called upon to find is known as informal research. You are not likely—though it is not impossible—to be called on to conduct formal research. The main difference between the two is the written description of the research process (a formal report) and findings typically shared with a broad audience. Research scientists write up their research methodology and findings in professional journals and other formal outlets. Graduate students write up their research in theses and dissertations. In the rare event you are called on to conduct formal research, remember this: Regardless the approach used to commit research to writing, the main elements of a research paper are as follows:

- *Title page*
- *Introduction.* This component of the research report should contain a specific, definitive identification of the problem researched. It is critical to define the problem as narrowly as possible so you do not allow irrelevant information to contaminate your research.
- *Literature review.* This component of the research report is a brief summary of the relevant information contained in journals, magazines, theses, dissertations, and other relevant written sources. The relevant information in each source is summarized in your report. This is typically the longest component of a research report.
- *Research methodology.* This component of your research report contains a comprehensive description of the methods you used in conducting the research. This is important because invalid methodologies result in invalid findings.
- *Data analysis.* This component of your research report explains your analysis of the research findings; how you interpret their meaning. This is the component in which honesty and integrity are the foremost considerations.

- *Results.* This component of the report is often the shortest, but it is nonetheless important. This component is where you describe what your findings mean as they relate to the research problem identified in the introduction. The results component contains the information required to state what the research has revealed.
- *Conclusion.* This component of the research report contains the *bottom line* of your findings. It answers the question: "What do the results of the research say about the issue in question?" It says, "From this research, I can conclude the following . . ."
- *References.* In conducting formal research, it is important to cite any sources you quote, paraphrase, or call out in your research. Failing to do so amounts to plagiarism. Further, the references cited make the report transparent in that they allow other researchers to check the validity of the research and replicate the research if necessary.

SUMMARY

There are times when even the most skilled critical thinker cannot sort through the deception, distortion, and lies of the "I think, I need, and I want" crowd. When this happens, the answer is good research.

- The elements of good research are honesty, integrity, transparency, and independence.
- Informal research—the kind you will most often be called on to conduct—involves reading professional journals relating to the issue in question, reading information posted on the internet (carefully and with an eye to bias), and seeking the advice of experts on the matter in question.
- Benefits of good research include the following: it adds to or clarifies the data relevant to a given issue, question, or

assertion; and it adds to the body of knowledge about a given topic.

- The value of good research goes beyond the two practical benefits; it does the following: promotes truth-telling, adds to the body of knowledge relating to a given topic generally and specifically, allows stakeholders to learn in ways that improve their decisions and subsequent actions, helps achieve a better understanding of issues, problems, and questions.
- Develops a valuable skill for aspiring critical thinkers, and ensures important decisions are based on up-to-date, accurate information.

7

DEATH OF THE TRUTH AND TRUST

You are lied to everyday. You are subjected to misinformation, distortions, and outright lies over social media, by politicians, in television ads, the internet, the news media, and other sources. If you are a college student, chances are high you are lied to by professors pushing a Marxist agenda. These platforms are pipelines for advancing nefarious agendas requiring bending, manipulation, and distortion of the truth. This is why we wrote this book. It is important that honest, right-minded people are able to sort through the fog of lies, distortion, and misinformation and recognize the truth, regardless the source of the input in question.

One of the most egregious examples of purposeful distortions can be seen on television and internet ads for pharmaceutical companies. They pay talented voice actors and use compelling images to encourage you to buy their drugs. Then in tones that make dying sound like a wonderful experience, they quietly list all the debilitating side effects, and this only because government regulations require them to do so. If you listen carefully, it's uncanny how many of the ill side effects of these drugs are the same. They treat "mild" effects the same as "may cause death."

Worse than television ads is the purposeful spread of lies over social media. Facebook, Twitter (now X), YouTube, Tik-Tok, and other social media platforms have become the favored misinformation tools for people with questionable agendas. They are used by politicians, the government, companies, individuals, and foreign governments to spread lies and in the case of foreign governments—particularly China and Russia—to create chaos in Western countries.

THREE CLASSES OF INFORMATION RECIPIENTS

The death of truth has led to the development of three classes of information recipients: naive sleepwalkers who believe everything they are exposed to, sheep who are intellectually weak, lazy, or mentally immature. The second group consists of self-centered liars who use social media and other platforms to manipulate and distort the truth to promote their nefarious agendas. This practice gave rise to the concept of "fake news." The final group consists of cautious doubters; critical thinkers who out of frustration with the lies, distortions, and manipulation of facts believe nothing they hear on television or read on social media. Rather, they check and double-check all input they receive.

An example of how self-centered liars operate is the anti-Semitic mobs that formed in the wake of the Hamas attacks on Israel. Well-indoctrinated, highly "educated" people ignored the facts because they did not suit their agenda, claiming Israel was the aggressor and the perpetrator of genocide. They made these ridiculous claims despite mountains of evidence to the contrary. Although Hamas made a point of documenting the rape, murders, and genocide it perpetrated and showed the evidence to the world, self-serving liars who supported Hamas denied these things ever happened.

WHAT HAS HAPPENED TO THE TRUTH?

We tend to think of the death of the truth as a new phenomenon but, in fact, it began in the garden of Eden when Satan lied to Eve and she believed him because his lie appealed to her more than God's truth. There is no question that lies, distortions, and manipulations are the result of self-centeredness, but the real cause is a much bigger concept. The death of truth is a result of the death of faith in God. People who accept Holy Scripture as the only real, enduring, and unchanging source of truth do not lie to promote self-interest. Turning to God is turning to the truth. Turning away from God is turning away from the truth.

DANGERS OF ARTIFICIAL INTELLIGENCE

The death of truth has been complicated further by the introduction of artificial intelligence (AI)—the ability to fabricate information and claim it is true. Some of the dangers of artificial intelligence include the following:

- *Abuse of intellectual property rights.* Skilled users of artificial intelligence can use the work of other people and make it appear to be theirs.
- *Disproportionate benefits.* Large corporations have the resources to take advantage of artificial intelligence while small businesses and individuals do not.
- *Difficulty in sorting out the truth.* Artificial intelligence makes it easier for bad actors to pass false information as the truth. This can lead to security breaches from sophisticated cyber-attacks. Artificial intelligence is likely to lead to increased abuse by foreign countries.
- *Proliferation of false and misleading information.* This is the biggest challenge critical thinkers face and the biggest

opportunity self-serving liars have when it comes to sorting out or distorting the truth.

Artificial intelligence just increases the importance of being a cautious questioner when it comes to information in the media or on social media. Check, double-check, and triple-check.

DEADLY LIES

Arguably, the deadliest result of a culture swamped in lies, deception, and coercion is how many have been detached from a once trusted healthcare system. It was already going downhill as politicians and insurance companies encroached evermore with regulations and control over doctors and hospitals.

Then came COVID-19. Mask and "vaccine" mandates overwhelmed our society like few things have in our lifetimes. The evidence is rolling out almost daily that the two things touted to be the devices to save us from this dreaded malady have perhaps caused as much trouble and illness as the Chinese made/spread virus.

Doctors, dentists, and opticians we long trusted with our health caved to the anti-science political pressure from Washington and their administrators. They forced everyone to wear masks in their offices and pushed the untested "vaccine." Well into 2023 masks were still being worn by those cowed by fear in public and some even while driving alone in the cars. Data now showing the health compromise masks can have on those who wear them makes one wonder what happened to the oath physicians take to "first, do not harm."

Obviously, there are still many in the medical field who deserve our trust as they diligently apply their knowledge and experience to the benefit of those in their care. And many stepped up during the COVID hysteria to speak reason and truth into the narrative. Unfortunately, however, a heavy blow has been dealt to a once revered profession, all because unscrupulous people took advantage of the opportunity to grab power and money. And again, administrators, not medically trained professionals, imposed deleterious policies on clinics and hospitals, endangering patients. We need business professionals to run hospitals so doctors can care for the sick and dying, but these businesspeople need to keep their hands off medicine.

For many, medical professionals can no longer be trusted. That will surely lead to a decline in the health of Americans. The agencies created to safeguard against health hazards of all kinds from the CDC (Centers for Disease Control) to the WHO (World Health Organization) have lost all or most of their credibility through the COVID outbreak. While suppressing the use of effective existing and inexpensive medications and pushing untested "vaccines," they fomented mass fear through mask mandates and group restrictions. What might happen when they next broadcast warnings about something real?

Needless to say, we must judge pharmaceutical companies harshly as they continue to roll out drug after drug. We must take responsibility for our own bodies and the problems we incur living in a fallen world and with entropy. Pray, research, and discern God's truth.

SUMMARY

It is more critical than ever for us to think objectively about everything going on around us. The devastating shift caused by COVID-19 has lasting detrimental impact on people around the world. Those who perpetuated it are not about to let us recover and return to normalcy. You can be sure the next medical crisis to be exploited by the workers of evil is on the horizon. We must be diligent to discern and apply truth to our lives on those around us. AI also looms as a black cloud of harm as it is used by those who continue to amass wealth and power over us.

- As a result of the internet and social media, lies from the enemy are ubiquitous and constant.

- There are basically three types of people in this miasma of lies and distortion. So-called sheep who simply stroll through their lives believing almost everything they see and hear.
- Then there are the liars who benefit from sowing deception, one class is known as "false news."
- Finally, there are those who refuse to take what they see and hear at face value. They think critically, analyze carefully, and reach wise conclusions.
- The narrative about AI (artificial intelligence) is heating up. Critical thinking on this topic is a matter of life and death.
- Perhaps the most dangerous result of COVID-19 is the fear spread throughout communities and nations leading to a shroud of doubt cast over the medical industry including pharmaceuticals.

8

SEPARATE FACTS FROM OPINIONS

*D*uring discussions of issues, questions, and proposals, some speakers will attempt to present their views as hard facts. They adopt an attitude of certainty, making it difficult to separate facts from fiction. Critical thinkers do not let themselves get sucked in by this strategy. In fact, the speaker's certainty and pushy attitude can be evidence of distortion, deception, or lies being used to advance an agenda. Does the phrase "he sounds a little too slick" ring a bell?

To begin, it is important to know the difference between facts and opinions. A fact is information subjected to rigorous scrutiny and proven to be true. An opinion is a belief, conviction, or sentiment one holds to be true. An exception to this definition occurs when advocates of a certain point of view make statements they know are not true to support their agenda. This is not an opinion; it is a lie.

There are obviously biased opinions and there are rational opinions. Not everyone who presents an opinion is trying to adversely influence listeners. A rational decision is one based on the latest information available on the topic in question, one that has prima facie credibility in the eyes of a reasonable person. A rational opinion should be given due consideration rather than rejected out of hand. An example of a rational opinion is French fries are bad for you. Since we all know French fries are fried in oil, it is possible this assertion is correct. Of course, it must still withstand the test of research which, by the way, will confirm the assertion that French fries are bad for you.

WHY IS IT IMPORTANT TO SEPARATE FACT FROM FICTION?

A good critical thinker knows how to analyze an issue from all sides, make rational judgements, and suppress personal preferences. This is important. Separating facts from opinion is an important skill for aspiring critical thinkers to learn. When you can separate facts from opinions, you are better able to communicate your point of view to an undecided audience. It even helps negate opposing points of view from people who are using distortion, deception, and lies in an attempt to advance an agenda.

Separating facts from opinions improves decisions at work, in sports, in education and most any other venue. Good decisions lead to positive, helpful solutions to problems and answers to questions. This, in turn, leads to better efficiency, productivity, and quality results. Let's look at an example from the workplace. One of the most common challenges faced by critical thinkers in the workplace is separating gossip from facts.

Employees congregate in the break room and it is not long before the rumors start. Rumors are unsubstantiated statements, usually about fellow employees, but they can be about anything such as possible layoffs, moving the company's facility to another location, or a pending merger. Anything that concerns employees will inevitably stoke the rumor mill.

An example of rumors about a fellow employee being used in an attempt to influence decision-makers occurs when an employee is rumored to be violating company policy by having an illicit affair with a colleague. This employee is married with two children and the company's policies are strongly pro-family. If the rumor is true, the employee will lose her job. Consequently, it is important for decision-makers to separate fact from fiction in this case. If the rumors persist, they could cost the employee not just her job, but her marriage too. Another example of rumors being spread in the workplace occurs when someone, often with an agenda, gets the rumor mill started and passes the rumor on to other employees.

Ben is unhappy with his employer because his best friend at work was just fired for professional ethics violations. As a result, he decides to spread a rumor about impending layoffs. Ben has a vengeance-oriented agenda. If the rumor catches on, perhaps some of the company's top performers will jump ship to save their careers. This is, of course, shortsighted on Ben's part. After all, undercutting his company's performance puts his own career at risk. Hurting the company could hurt him. But Ben is part of the "I think, I feel, and I want" crowd. Consequently, shooting himself in the foot in response to a perceived problem is an acceptable response in his eyes.

METHODS FOR SEPARATING FACTS FROM OPINIONS

Separating facts from opinions requires critical thinkers to examine the issue from all sides and make rational inferences while avoiding personal judgments that might bias their analysis. There are several methods for separating facts from opinions. These methods are explained in this section.

- *Don't be drawn in by flowery adjectives.* An adjective is a word that modifies or describes a noun. A noun is a word that describes a person, place, or thing. Consider this statement: *This excellent report is critical to our future.* This excellent report is critical to our future. In this statement, "report" is the noun; "excellent" and "critical" are adjectives chosen to give the report credibility in the minds of listeners. They are flowery terms chosen to influence listeners and, perhaps, have them overlook shortcomings in the report. An appropriate response to this statement about a report is to ask what makes the report "excellent" and "critical." A maxim in critical thinking is there is a direct correlation between how many adjectives are used in making a presentation or presenting a point of view and how many nouns. The more nouns and the fewer adjectives the better. Flowery adjectives include such terms as *good, new, first, great, right, high, large, important, critical,* and *substantial.*

- ***Play devil's advocate.*** An effective technique when trying to sort facts out from opinions is to play devil's advocate. You present the opposite side of his argument then summarize the opposite side for listeners. Present your idea as a way to strengthen his argument as well as to identify holes in it. An even more effective technique is to ask presenters to play devil's advocate. Honest presenters will look for holes in their argument as steadfastly as you would. But presenters with an agenda will studiously avoid the obvious problems with their proposal or assertions. When presenters avoid obvious concerns, you know you are dealing with a weak argument being advanced by a member of the "I think, I feel, and I want" crowd.

- ***Apply logic.*** It is important to sort out facts from opinions, but doing so is a first step, not a solution. Facts, by themselves, do not necessarily tell the whole story about the issue in question. Before drawing conclusions based solely on the facts discovered about a proposal or assertion, ask yourself, "Is what we know about this situation logical?" Facts can be cherry-picked to fit an argument or agenda. In other words, facts—though true—can be chosen selectively to support an assertion or give validity to a proposal. If you think presenters are cherry-picking their facts, ask them to explain their conclusion while pointing out facts that are being avoided. For example, say a colleague at work is pushing a new project. He claims the project will be financially advantageous to the company and will allow the company to finish the year in a good financial position. While these assertions are true—they are facts—they do not tell the whole story. Another relevant fact is the community is organizing to protest the project and the word on the street is the protests could become violent.

- *Maintain a positive attitude.* Maintaining a positive attitude in discussions of assertions or proposals is important. If you have a combative attitude or one that is overly aggressive you might cause presenters to become defensive and attack back or continue to support their conclusions when they might otherwise have been swayed by a calmer opponent. Mindy was an aggressive advocate for her point of view no matter how trivial the argument might be. She was known to tell presenters, "That's nonsense and you know it" or "Get serious." As a result, not only did the presenters she attacked become hardened in their opinions, other listeners gravitated to the presenter's argument out of empathy.

LEARN TO INTERPRET NONVERBAL COMMUNICATION

Critical thinkers are good at reading nonverbal cues, what is often referred to as body language. There are seminars galore on how to read nonverbal cues, but the truth is you do not need a seminar. You have been able to read nonverbal cues since you were a baby. A child can tell when his mother is tense, angry, or sad. You are more capable of reading nonverbal cues than a baby. All you have to do is focus on the presenter and pay attention. A maxim in communication is "body language speaks louder than words." People often communicate through physical behavior, mannerisms, and facial expressions without even knowing it. This fact gives critical thinkers a powerful tool for separating facts from opinions. For example, if presenters make claims but cannot look you in the eyes, they may be lying and you will want to dig deeper into their claim.

ROLES NONVERBAL COMMUNICATION CAN PLAY IN DISCUSSIONS

Nonverbal cues can play several roles in communication.

- The first is *confirmation*. It can support and confirm the message as being true. This happens when the verbal and the nonverbal messages match. Nonverbal cues can also contradict the message. If the nonverbal cues do not match the verbal message, the presenter may be lying. Let us suppose a presenter makes a claim about a product he is trying to sell, but he cannot look you in the eyes or his hands shake, he may be lying and you will want to dig deeper into his claims.
- *Replacement* is the next role nonverbal cues can play. Replacement means body language is used to convey the message in the place of a verbal message. For example, if you ask a friend if she knows what movie is playing at the theater, she might just shrug instead answering verbally. The shrug would convey the same message as "I don't know."
- *Complementing* is another role nonverbal cues can play. Complementing means adding to or supporting the verbal message. For example, in football when someone makes a good play or in baseball when someone gets a hit, his teammates do not stop at just saying "good job," they also give the player a high five or a pat on the back. These nonverbal cues add to or complement the words.
- *Reinforcing* is the final role nonverbal cues can play. Nonverbal cues can reinforce the verbal message. For example, assume your boss at work is angry about the lack of productivity from your team. She calls a team meeting and gives the

members a good chewing out. In the middle of her diatribe, she slams her fist on the table to emphasize her anger. This is nonverbal reinforcement of the verbal message.

TYPES OF NONVERBAL COMMUNICATION

There are several different types of nonverbal communication aspiring critical thinkers should be familiar with. These include facial expressions, posture or body poses, hand gestures, eye contact, touch, proximity, and tone of voice.

- Facial expressions give away a lot when it comes to communication. By observing facial expressions, you can detect happiness, sadness, anger, frustration, surprise, fear, and disgust. Further, facial expressions are the same in all cultures and human backgrounds.
- Posture or body poses include how people sit, walk, hold their head, stand, or move. One of the most common body poses in to cross one's arms as a sign of disagreement. Another example is sitting casually rather than formally or rigidly. One conveys a message of confidence and the other a message of tenseness or uncertainty. In his race for the presidency way back in 1960, Richard Nixon is thought to have lost votes because in a televised interview with him and his opponent, John F. Kennedy, Nixon slouched in his chair. His body posture conveyed a message of disinterest and a lack of respect for the interview. Kennedy, on the other hand, sat up straight and more formally conveyed a message of respect for the process and interest in the interview.
- Hand gestures can convey nonverbal cues. Pointing at someone aggressively, for example, can convey a threatening message. Using your hands to emphasize the message can also convey nonverbal cues. People will spread their hands during a conversation to convey sincerity for example. Of

course, the gesture can be used by people with an agenda to convey false sincerity.

- Eye contact is one of the most telling ways of conveying nonverbal cues. The eyes can convey such messages as hostility, anger, and interest. If they look for no other nonverbal cues, critical thinkers observe the eyes of presenters.
- Touch is another telling way to convey nonverbal cues. The most often given example of this is the nonverbal cues a handshake can convey. A limp handshake can convey a message of weakness and uncertainty. A bone-crushing handshake conveys a message of aggression and bullying. A firm but not bone-crushing handshake augmented by the individual looking you in the eyes conveys confidence and certainty.
- Proximity can convey powerful messages. Getting too close to other people can convey a message of either aggression or intimacy. It involves getting in their space which could be welcomed or off-putting depending on the relationship or circumstances.
- Tone of voice is one of the most telling sources of nonverbal cues. How you say what you have to say makes a big difference. Is it said in a calm and confident voice, a shrill and frantic voice, or a reluctant and hesitant voice? How loud are your words and how are they paced? An individual who speaks too fast, for example, will appear to be in a hurry to get it all out before someone questions or challenges her.

FAKING NONVERBAL COMMUNICATION

The most committed members of the "I think, I feel, and I want" crowd often try to fake nonverbal communication to support their proposals or assertions. Fortunately, it is more difficult to fake nonverbal communication than verbal communication. Nonetheless, there are books and seminars widely available that teach people how to use nonverbal communication to their advantage. In other words, to fake it. They might teach you to hold eye contact when presenting your message or to stand a certain way. The problem with faking nonverbal communication is many of the nonverbal cues people give off are not controllable, they are automatic; we often do not know we are sending nonverbal cues. People who try to fake nonverbal communication will appear stiff and uncomfortable as if they are forcing the issue.

EMOTIONS IN NONVERBAL COMMUNICATION

When trying to sort out facts from opinions it is important to consider the role emotions can play. Appealing to your emotions is one of the favorite tactics of people pushing an agenda. This is why it is important to remain objective during discussions of issues. Objectivity will help you see through the rhetoric to the actual issues. As an aspiring critical thinker, you need to be able to recognize the emotions of presenters as well as your own emotions. Emotional awareness will help you do the following:

- Read the nonverbal cues people give off by observing their emotions. This will help you get a more accurate picture of the situation. Are they excited, uncertain, tense, rigid, happy, sad, or angry? All these emotions can skew the message in one direction or the other. Nonverbal cues can send a message of trust by matching the verbal message being conveyed. They can also show others you are tuned in and not to be fooled by nonverbal cues or verbal messages.

COMMUNICATING EFFECTIVELY WITH THOSE WHOSE OPINIONS YOU REJECT

Communicating with people you disagree with can be difficult. It is a challenge to disagree with someone without them taking offense or becoming defensive. However, aspiring critical thinkers must learn to communicate effectively with the opposition for the good of the decisions that are eventually made. To improve communication with the opposition, try the following tactics:

- **Disagree without being disagreeable.** Remember to maintain a positive relationship with the opposition; you might need them to support your proposals in the future. Avoid harsh words or accusations. Instead, use phrases such as "I see your point, but have you considered this . . ." or "I can tell you have put a lot of work into your presentation, but can we consider these points . . ."
- **Control your emotions.** Do not allow yourself to become angry, frustrated, or offended. Your emotions will influence the presenter whether they are positive or negative. Controlling your emotions prevents the presenter from becoming defensive and makes it harder to lose control of emotions.
- **Do not back down but be humble.** When dealing with people, a little humility goes a long way. Boisterous, pushy people are not usually effective at winning others to their point of view. Humble people make it difficult for a presenter to use such tactics as aggressive hand gestures, intimidating body language, anger, and other negative tactics.
- **Try to understand the presenter's point of view.** Even when you do not accept it, try to understand the presenter's point of view. Where is she coming from? You can do this by paraphrasing the presenter's assertions and echoing them back to her. Understanding where the presenter is coming from will help you find the holes in her argument.
- **Look for common ground with the opposition.** Even when you disagree with a presenter, you may be able to find common ground. Even the smallest amount of common ground gives you something to build on. It also lets the presenter off the hook by showing he might be at least partially right.

SUMMARY

During discussions of issues, questions, and proposals, some people will present their opinions as facts. Consequently, it is important for aspiring critical thinkers to avoid being sucked in by opinions stated as facts.

- A good critical thinker knows how to analyze an issue from all sides, make rational judgments, and avoid allowing personal preference to enter the process. This is an important skill because when you distinguish between facts and opinions, you are better able to communicate your point of view to an undecided audience.
- Separating facts from opinions improves decisions at work, in sports, in education, and in any other venue. Good decisions based on facts lead to positive, helpful solutions to problems and better answers to questions.
- Methods to avoid being drawn in by assertively stated opinions include the following: 1) Do not be drawn in by flowery adjectives such as *great*, *wonderful*, *one-of-a-kind*, *the best*, and other over-the-top adjectives. There is a direct correlation between how many adjectives are used in a presentation and how many nouns. The more nouns and the fewer adjectives the better.
- Playing the devil's advocate will help you separate facts from opinions. Ask presenters to turn their argument upside down and present the other side. If they are unwilling to do this, you do it. Honest presenters will be willing to look for holes in their proposals while those who are pushing an agenda or are lying will not.
- Applying logic is helpful in sorting out facts from opinions. Logic is sound reasoning. It is important because facts, by themselves, do not necessarily tell the whole story. Facts can be selectively chosen and selectively left out. Because of this, it is important for aspiring critical thinkers to apply logic to

the facts presented by asking, "Does this make sense?" and "Is this information complete?"

- Maintaining a positive attitude will keep the discussion flowing and ensure the opposition does not go into defensive mode. A combative, aggressive attitude will just harden the opposition. It will also turn others in the audience against you.
- Critical thinkers are good at reading nonverbal cues, sometimes referred to as body language. Nonverbal communication can play several roles in presentations of ideas, assertions, and proposals. The roles include the following: 1) confirmation of the message, 2) replacement (using body language to replace verbal messages), and 3) complementing the verbal message (using body language to support the message.)
- There are several different types of body language that give nonverbal cues. These include facial expressions, posture or body poses, hand gestures, eye contact, touch, proximity, and tone of voice.
- Some people try to fake nonverbal communication. Fortunately, it is difficult to do. Most nonverbal cues are done without a person thinking about them. They are automatic. Consequently, when people try to fake nonverbal communication, they appear as awkward.
- It is important for critical thinkers to avoid letting their emotions cloud the issue being discussed and to observe the emotions of presenters. Doing so will ensure you get a more accurate picture of the issue.
- Communicating effectively with those who oppose your opinion can be difficult. It is always a challenge. Nonetheless, it is important to learn this critical thinking skill. To improve communication with the opposition, here are some strategies: 1) disagree without being disagreeable, 2) control your emotions, 3) do not back down but be humble, 4) try to understand the opposition's point of view even though you do not accept it, and 5) look for common ground between you and the opposition.

9

APPLY COMMON SENSE

One of the best tools for aspiring critical thinkers is the application of common sense. So, what do we mean by common sense? Common sense consists of widely known facts about the world most human beings are supposed to know. For example, telling someone who fell and injured his knee to see a doctor is the application of common sense—something most people should know.

Logic and common sense complement each other but they are not the same thing. Logic amounts to using knowledge and reason to analyze the input you receive. For example, the thermometer reads thirty-one degrees Fahrenheit. Logic tells us it is cold outside and we should bundle up before leaving the house. Common sense, on the other hand, requires no analysis. Rather it depends on the application of knowledge widely known and accepted. In the example just given, common sense would tell us to bundle up without having to even think about it.

Common sense is often based on the human senses of touch, sight, hearing, smell, and taste. Your senses send messages to the brain that help to perceive the world around you. Applying this knowledge is common sense. Common sense is why you sometimes have the feeling something is wrong or missing in an argument, but cannot quite put your finger on what it is. It just feels wrong.

EXAMPLES OF COMMON SENSE

Let's look at several examples of common sense. Common sense tells us to use an umbrella when it is raining, to put on oven mitts when handling a hot dish, look both ways before crossing the street, obey the speed limit, dress up for a job interview, be respectful when pulled over by the police for speeding, obey your employer's personnel policies, wait to enter an elevator until others have exited, and turn off your cell phone during a job interview. All these examples have one thing in common: they are based on either widely known knowledge or what should be widely known. People who violate these common-sense rules give rise to the maxim "common sense is not so common these days."

REFUTING FALSE ARGUMENTS

It is important for aspiring critical thinkers to recognize false arguments; arguments that fly in the face of common sense. There are numerous kinds of false arguments you should become familiar with. Each is explained in this section.

- *The "look who is talking" argument.* With this argument, the individual in question claims she should be excused from taking appropriate action because the person recommending it is guilty of the same thing. For example, suppose someone claims you should cut back on fatty foods to lower your cholesterol. If you respond with "I'll quit when you quit. You eat more fatty foods than I do." You have just made the "look who is talking" argument. Just because the other individual is guilty of the same behavior does not mean you should continue your inappropriate behavior.

- *The sidetracking argument.* This argument is sometimes referred to as the red herring argument. It involves raising irrelevant issues and then claiming those issues settle the original argument. For example, claiming an automobile manufacturer should stop all production because one of its models has a safety problem. By quoting safety statistics, the presenter claims he has validated the original argument. But this is a red herring. The manufacturer might stop production of the model in question until the safety problem is corrected, but production of the other models without the problem should be continued.

- *The strawman argument.* With this argument, the presenter distorts and inaccurately paraphrases your argument to weaken it and then questions the weaker version. For example, assume you are arguing that to save Medicare and Social Security, the age of eligibility should be increased to seventy years of age. The presenter offers a strawman argument in which he claims you want to eliminate Medicare and Social Security. Then he attacks your argument from that perspective.

- *The ad hominem argument.* With this argument, the person making the presentation or the person opposing it is attacked personally while ignoring the merits of his argument. The ad hominem argument has become a mainstay in contemporary politics. It was seen at its worst during the confirmation hearings for Supreme Court justices Clarence Thomas and Neil Gorsuch. Both nominees, and other conservative nominees to the high court, were subjected to brutal false accusations by Leftist ideologues. The attacks on these highly qualified individuals were picked up, endorsed, and spread by the mainstream media. The ad hominem argument is what undercuts Donald Trump's popularity with certain voters. His tendency to attack anyone who disagrees with him turns off a lot of voters who admire his policies and would, otherwise, be in his camp.

- *Appeal to authority argument.* With this argument, the views of so-called authorities are offered as proving the presenter's assertions. The problem with this argument is the authorities cited often are false authorities. You see this in commercial ads all the time. Companies advertising their products hire well-known actors and actresses to be spokespeople for their products when, in fact, these celebrities know nothing about the products. News anchors in the mainstream media are often cited as authorities when, in reality, they know little or nothing about what they are reporting. They just authoritatively read text someone else has prepared for them.

- *The whole-versus-parts argument.* With this argument, presenters posit what is true of the whole must be true of the parts. For example, a presenter might claim men are generally faster than women so it follows Ricky is faster than Jane. The whole in this case is the entire population of women. The part is an individual woman. The argument is obviously false. Jane could be faster than Ricky regardless of women in general being slower. The only way to test this false argument is to arrange a race between Ricky and Jane.

- *Bait-and-switch argument.* With this argument a term critical to the presenter's assertion is used in two different ways. Then the difference is used to validate the argument. The original use of the term is the bait. The second use of the term is the switch. For example, one might posit that soil is organic and organic things are good for you. Therefore, it is good to eat dirt. In this case, the term critical to the presenter's assertion is soil. In one instance it is used as an organic substance. In the other instance, it is used as dirt. The success of the presenter's assertion depends on the audience accepting the claim that because something is organic it is automatically good for you.

- *Everyone-believes-it argument.* With this argument, the presenter attempts to validate her assertion based on the popularity of her claim. A popular view held by a lot of people is, in the eyes of the presenter, sufficient validation of her assertion. The problem with this argument is popularity does not necessarily correlate with truth. Remember what was stated in the first chapter: If something is false, it is false no matter how many people believe it. Something can be widely believed but false. At one time, the majority of people in the world believed the earth was flat. There was a time when smoking was widely considered good for you. This fallacious claim was based on the advertisements of cigarette manufacturers, not scientific research.

- *Appeal-to-history argument.* With this argument, the presenter claims that because something has been believed for a long time it must be valid. This is similar to the everyone-believes-it argument except it is based on history rather than popularity. For example, people have believed in Unidentified Flying Objects or UFOs for a long time. Therefore, UFOs must be real. UFOs may indeed be real, but if they are it is not because people have believed in them for a long time.

- *Not-proven argument.* With this argument, presenters claim something must be true because it has not been proven false. It can also be posited using this argument that something must be false because it has not been proven true. For example, a presenter might claim there is life on Mars. His validation of this claim is no one has proven there is not life on Mars. The argument can also be flipped. It must be false because no one has proven there is life on Mars. Either way, the argument is invalid. Whether there is or is not life on Mars is not true or false because of the lack of proof. We will know whether there is life on Mars only after a space mission to Mars has brought back evidence one way or the other.

- *Appeal-to-emotion argument.* With this argument, presenters try to engage the listener's compassion, pity, or sympathy, although these feelings are not relevant to the discussion. For example, a lackluster employee has missed several days of work with no explanation. When called on the carpet by her boss, she attempts to illicit sympathy by claiming, "I had to take care of my mother. She is sick" when, in fact, she was having a little water-skiing vacation with friends from college who showed up unannounced. Another example of the appeal-to-emotion argument is the college student who asks the professor to overlook the fact he has not completed the course assignment because he might flunk out otherwise.

- *False dilemma argument.* With this argument, the presenter posits two possible scenarios then states only one of them can be true. Hence, the one she favors must be true. A literary critic might posit a best-selling author wrote all his books by himself or he might posit a ghost writer wrote them. There is evidence the best-selling author did not write some of his books. Therefore, a ghost writer must have written all of them. This scenario is the one favored by the literary critic who is no fan of the best-selling author. This is a false dilemma because the best-selling author might have written some of his books and a ghost writer might have written some of them.

- *The slippery slope argument.* With this argument, the presenter claims you should not take a first step because it will inevitably lead to a second, third, and fourth step, all of which could have undesirable outcomes. Here is an example of the slippery slope argument. You tell a friend you are going to skip your workouts at the gym this week. He counters, "You'd better not. If you do you will lose momentum and stop going to the gym at all. Then you will gain weight and begin to have heart problems. Before you know it, you will be in the hospital. You could die of a heart attack or stroke." This is a false argument because skipping a week at the gym does not mean you will never go back to the gym.

In fact, a week of rest and rejuvenation might actually do you some good.

- *False conclusion argument.* With this argument, the presenter draws a conclusion based on biased or incomplete information. For example, the presenter who loves to eat fatty foods such as fried chicken or barbecued pork claims, "There is no risk in eating these kinds of food. My mother-in-law ate them all her life and lived to be ninety years old." This is a false conclusion because her mother-in-law is a sample of one. A larger sample might well suggest a different conclusion.

- *False analogies argument.* With this argument, the presenter draws a conclusion based on a false comparison between two or more non-analogous things. For example, a friend might tell you, "I am going to buy a new navy-blue suit for my job interview because I was wearing a navy-blue suit when I got my last two jobs. It has worked twice now, so I know it will work again." This is a false analogy because wearing a navy-blue suit and having a successful interview are not analogous. The presenter might have gotten his two previous jobs because he had an excellent resume or just the right experience and education the employer was looking for.

- *Inaccurate conclusion argument.* With this argument, someone who opposes an assertion claims that because part of the information presented is inaccurate the conclusion is invalid. While it is true the conclusion may be invalid, this is not necessarily the case. It might just mean the presenter needs to do more homework and find better information to support his assertion. For example, a fellow college student tells you, "It's okay to skip a few classes. Everyone does it." The inaccurate conclusion, "everyone does it" means it is acceptable when, in fact, it just means it is a popular thing to do. As we have already seen in this section just because something is popular does not mean it is right or advisable.

The student asking for advice would do well to look into his fellow student's assertion everyone does it. Is this claim really true? Further, even if everybody does it, it does not validate the practice. It would also be wise to determine what happens to students who skip classes.

- *False causation argument.* With this argument, the presenter confuses correlation with causation. This argument ignores the possibility of coincidence or other relevant factors. She assumes one action caused a specific result when, in fact, the result could be attributed to other factors. For example, a high school student brings his teacher a cake on her birthday. On his next essay, he receives an "A" for a grade. He draws the inaccurate conclusion, based on false causation, he got an "A" because he buttered up the teacher with a birthday cake when, in fact, he might have done a good job writing his essay.

- *False compromise argument.* With this argument, the presenter thinks finding a middle-ground compromise between opposing points of view equates to a valid conclusion. This argument overlooks two important facts. First, a compromise solution might just be a marriage of two invalid options. Second, there might be better solutions available than the compromise solution.

- *False complexity argument.* With this argument, a stakeholder claims that because the issue is too complex for her to grasp it must be false. The problem with this argument is whether people can or cannot understand an issue does not mean it is false. For example, a lot of people do not understand calculus, but that does not mean calculus is an invalid form of mathematics. A colleague who claims, "I don't understand our new marketing strategy so I am going to stick with the old methods," is using the false complexity argument.

- The bad news for aspiring critical thinkers is that there are a lot of false arguments to be aware of. The good news is they can all be recognized and rejected by applying common sense. Calling on your experience, knowledge, and insight, you can determine when something about an argument does not feel right. When this is the case, your common sense is working and you know additional inquiry is in order.

SUMMARY

One of the best tools for aspiring critical thinkers is the application of common sense. Common sense consists of widely known facts you have learned from experience, research, observation, or any other source.

- Logic and common sense complement each other but are not the same thing. Logic involves applying reason to analyze facts. Common sense requires no analysis. Rather it amounts to sensing when something is amiss based on what you know to be true.
- Common sense tells us to use an umbrella when it is raining, to put on oven mitts when handling hot dishes, to obey the speed limit, dress up for an interview, be respectful when pulled over by a police officer for speeding, obey your employer's personnel policies, wait to enter an elevator until others have exited, and turn off your cell phone during a job interview. We don't have to even think about situations like these because common sense tells us what to do or not to do.
- Common sense is often based on the human senses of touch, sight, hearing, smell, and taste. Your senses send messages to the brain that help you perceive the world around you. Common sense is why you sometimes sense something is wrong with the input you receive, but cannot quite put your finger on it.
- There are a lot of false arguments people use to advance an agenda or gain acceptance of an invalid point of view. These

include the following: "look-who-is-talking" argument, sidetracking argument, strawman argument, ad hominem argument, appeal-to-authority argument, whole-versus-parts argument, bait-and-switch argument, everyone-believes-it argument, appeal-to-history argument, not-proven argument, appeal-to-emotion argument, false dilemma argument, slippery slope argument, false conclusion argument, false analogies argument, inaccurate conclusion argument, false causation argument, false compromise argument, and false complexity argument.

- The bad news is there are a lot false arguments that aspiring critical thinkers need to be familiar with. The good news is all these arguments can be recognized and rejected by applying common sense. Calling on your knowledge, experience, and insight when something about an argument does not feel right is the application of common sense. If it does not feel right, more investigation is in order.

10

RECOGNIZE AND REJECT AD HOMINEM ARGUMENTS

*T*he ad hominem argument involves conducting personal attacks on individuals rather than their arguments or assertions. It is the worst, most unethical strategy of the "I think, I need, and I want" crowd. The goal of the ad hominem argument is to invalidate a person's assertions by invalidating the person. Leftist ideologues use the ad hominem argument to prevent conservative judges from being approved by the Senate as Supreme Court Justices. Their false claims against the character and worthiness of two imminently qualified individuals were despicable.

As was seen in the Senate hearings for Justices Clarence Thomas and Neil Gorsuch, the ad hominem argument often amounts to falsely attacking an individual's character to make him appear unworthy of trust. An ad hominem attack might take the form of simple name calling or it might involve questioning the integrity, character, and motives of the individual in question. In recent years, the latter approach has become the favorite strategy of the Left.

In the case of Clarence Thomas, the Left accused him of having an illicit affair and being a racist (Justice Thomas is black). In an appalling example of hypocrisy, the Left criticized Thomas for being married to a white woman. Since his hearings in the Senate, the Left has continued its attacks on Justice Thomas. For example, they repeatedly claim he plagiarizes his opinions.

In the case of Neil Gorsuch, Leftist ideologues accused him of being a stooge of the rich and well-connected as well as being anti-worker, and pro-corporate in his decisions. Because this strategy is so destructive, it is important for aspiring critical thinkers to recognize and reject ad hominem arguments.

WHY AD HOMINEM ARGUMENTS ARE INHERENTLY FALSE

Ad hominem arguments focusing on the character or worthiness of the person making an argument rather than the argument itself are inherently false. The ad hominem argument is an invalid strategy because even if the individual making the argument is unworthy, she might still be right. Other reasons ad hominem arguments are invalid include the following: 1) they have nothing to do with the issue in question, 2) they are intended to shift the focus away from relevant information that contradicts the presenter's assertions, and 3) they base their validity on the false belief that attacking the source of an argument amounts to refuting the argument.

The following examples will demonstrate why ad hominem arguments are inherently false. Assume you question a colleague at work about his proposal to change a certain procedure. Rather than respond to your questions with logic and reason, he claims, "You are the most stubborn person I've ever met. You are against any change no matter how good it is."

Consider another example. A husband and wife are discussing buying a new car. The wife insists on a certain make and model, but the husband wants a more "manly" car. The discussion soon devolves into an argument. The husband yells at his wife, "What do you know about cars. You're not a mechanic. You don't know what you are talking about!"

A final example is two friends discussing a medical procedure. One says, "I just read an article in a medical journal claiming a new procedure is just what you need. The other individual, who does not want to undergo any medical procedure, responds, "You're not a doctor. What do you know?"

KINDS OF AD HOMINEM ARGUMENTS

There are several kinds of ad hominem arguments aspiring critical thinkers should be aware of; all of which represent a different way to attack someone with an opposing point of view. The names of the different kinds of ad hoc arguments sometimes vary from scholar to scholar, but regardless what any one individual calls them, they are the same kind of attack. The most common types of ad hominem arguments are explained in this section.

QUALIFICATIONS ARGUMENT

With this argument, the individual with an opposing view is attacked on the basis of professional qualifications. The most common version of this kind of ad hominem attack is, "You don't know what you are talking about. You aren't qualified to comment." Consider this example of the qualification argument. Lisa Jones is a nurse with thirty-five years' experience. She has been assigned to a case in which the physician in charge is stumped. The procedures and treatments he recommended so far are not working.

This physician is a rookie having just completed his residency. He also suffers from an overly inflated ego. When Lisa suggests a treatment she has seen work numerous times, the rookie physician attacks her claiming, "What do you know? You're a nurse, not a physician. Until you're a graduate of medical school, I don't want to hear your suggestions." As a result, a treatment that probably would have worked went untried.

FALSE MOTIVES ARGUMENT

With this argument, the motives of the individual with an opposing argument are dismissed as false, self-serving, or otherwise invalid. Greg and Micah are discussing the military budget. Greg, who has no plans to join the military and is a frequent anti-war protestor, claims, "You just want more funding for the military because you are going to enlist. If you weren't enlisting in the Army, you wouldn't support more funding for defense." This argument is obviously false since an individual can support increased defense spending without being in the military. Many people do.

POISONING-THE-WELL ARGUMENT

With this argument, the presenter attempts to discredit opponents by making false negative claims about them. For example, Marcus Alexander is a political scientist who often debates Leftwing ideologues on the issues of the day. In a recent debate, Marcus challenged his opponent's stand on security at our southern border. His opponent claimed the borders should remain open to all because America is a nation of immigrants. Marcus responded that the immigrants who came to America at an earlier time and passed through Ellis Island were not criminals and they entered our country legally. His opponent claimed "You are a racist. You would support immigration if those who are crossing our borders were white Europeans." He used the poisoning-the-well argument.

HYPOCRISY ARGUMENT

With this argument, the presenter attempts to discredit those who oppose his point of view by claiming they are hypocrites. He claims their argument is inconsistent with their past input. Therefore, they are hypocrites and have no credibility. Susan Morgan was a highly qualified engineer, but she had an ego problem that often led her to use the various arguments explained in this section in debates with colleagues. In a recent team meeting, a colleague suggested several changes to her design of a multi-story condominium. Susan's response was swift and biting. "Hypocrite! Last week you said just the opposite." She chose to use the hypocrisy argument.

CONNECTIONS ARGUMENT

With this argument, presenters try to invalidate the input of opponents by claiming they have a connection to something unrelated to the issue in question. In a classroom discussion at the local community college, Brian Mosher spoke in favor of reparations for minorities who could trace their lineage to slaves. Julie Brown challenged his claim with a question: "Why should people who never owned slaves pay reparations to people who have never been slaves?" Brian, clearly angered to be challenged, "It's no wonder you think like you do. You're probably a secret member of the Ku Klux Klan or some other white supremacy group." In making this statement, Brian tried to falsely connect Julie to groups that would undermine her credibility.

DO-NOT-CRITICIZE ARGUMENT

With this argument, the presenter claims people should simply avoid situations they oppose. For example, Jeff has no patience with people who oppose his point of view on any subject.

Recently at a family gathering, the subject of crime in our country came up. Jeff, who is an outspoken supporter of defunding the police, claimed, "The police are worse than the criminals. Besides, crime is overly hyped by the media." His brother-in-law responded, "You won't feel that way when you are mugged on the street." Jeff reacted in typical fashion. He told his brother-in-law, "If you don't like where things are in our country, why don't you move to another country." In other words, do not criticize. Do something, no matter how unrealistic, to avoid the unwanted situation rather than correcting it.

The absurdity of this argument is obvious. Jeff's brother-in-law is a citizen of the United States, has a home and family here, and is building a good career. He has every right to be concerned about the growing crime wave in our country and to criticize those who think police are the problem. If every person who is concerned about the direction of our country were to pack up and leave, we would lose half of the population, and it would be the wrong half.

TONE-OF-VOICE ARGUMENT

With this argument, the presenter challenges anyone who opposes his assertions based on their tone of voice rather than their point of view. The goal is to invalidate their argument by pointing out their offensive tone of voice; even if it is not offensive. The strategy aims to get others focused on something other than a weak argument. This happened to Marge Pureno during a PTO meeting. Another PTO member, Dick Smith, proposed the school consider a four-day school week. Marge opposed his view claiming it would create a hardship on working parents who would have to put their kids in daycare on Fridays. Dick, seeing several other members of the PTO nodding in agreement with Marge, immediately implemented the tone-of-voice argument. "You don't have to get so worked up about it, Marge. Why do you have to be so emotional about these things?" Fortunately, his strategy did not work. Another member of the

PTO claimed, "Dick, you are the only one in this room who is worked up. Marge's argument was calm, cool, and rational."

RESPONDING TO AD HOMINEN ARGUMENTS

In today's culture of wokeness, you are going to be subjected to ad hominem arguments. The "I think, I need, and I want" crowd will go to any length to be right and to have their assertions validated by others. When this happens, truth gets lost in the shuffle unless critical thinkers speak up. Consequently, it is important for aspiring critical thinkers to know how to respond to ad hominem arguments. Effective methods for doing so are explained in this section.

CHALLENGE THE ATTACK DIRECTLY

Do not just brush off ad hominem attacks. Confront them directly, but control your emotions. Be calm, confident, humble, respectful, and self-assured. In other words, be what the attacker is not. You know the attacks are false. Point out why. Also point out the attack is irrelevant because, even if everything said by the presenter is accurate, it has no bearing on the truth of your argument. For example, assume you just challenged a presenter's assertion that the new pitch clock and electronic strike zone are hurting major league baseball. The presenter, who approves of the changes, fires back, "You never played baseball so what do you know?" You might calmly respond, "I don't need to have played the game to have an opinion. I am a fan of major league baseball and know the rules inside out. I think these new rules change the whole character of the game."

EXPLAIN THE ATTACK IS IRRELEVANT

Ad hominem attacks are typically irrelevant. What an angry presenter says about someone who opposes her assertions has nothing to do with the validity of the opposing argument. The person challenging the presenter's assertions might indeed be a bad actor, but that does not mean she is wrong. For example, assume Theresa has a reputation for coming to work late. When she challenges a member of her work team's assertions about a new procedure he recommends they adopt, he attacks her claiming, "What do know about it. You can't even get to work on time. Why should we listen to you?" Theresa might calmly and confidently respond, "Whether I come to work on time or not is irrelevant to what you are proposing. My argument is valid regardless when I come to work."

BRUSH OFF THE ATTACK

With this argument, the presenter is attempting to do what ad hominem attackers always try to do: get the audience sidetracked so they do not focus on the weakness of his argument. An effective technique for countering an ad hominem attack is to simply make note of it and move on—brush it off. A demonstration of confidence on your part can speak louder than words. For example, in a departmental meeting of the English faculty at a large university, a faculty member proposes the department begin using the politically-correct pronouns recommended by the woke crowd. Another faculty member challenges his recommendation claiming, "Our job is not to give in to fallacious trends. It is to teach students how to enjoy, understand, and interpret good literature." The presenter, clearly angered, shot back, "Here we go again. Our in-house Nazi opposes anything that is progressive." You might acknowledge the insult by responding in a way that points out the absurdity of his comment. Here is an example of such a comment: "Your response is noted. I will let Hitler know how you feel." Then you simply brush it off and move on. The message you send with this approach is "your views of me are irrelevant. The rest of the faculty knows I am conservative, but not a Nazi."

SUMMARY

- With ad hominem arguments, an *individual* is attacked rather than his point of view or assertions. It is the worst, most unethical form of deception, distortion, and lying used by the "I think, I feel, and I want" crowd. The goal of the ad hominem argument is to invalidate a person's assertions by invalidating the person. Two well-known examples of using the ad hominem argument in this way are the Senate confirmation hearings for Justices Clarence Thomas and Neil Gorsuch to serve on the Supreme Court. Both men were vilified by the Left. Both men had their characters viciously attacked. Both men had their personal lives smeared by ad hominem attacks. The same approach has been used on other conservative Supreme Court nominees.
- Ad hominem attacks are inherently false because they have nothing to do with the issue in question, they are intended to shift the focus away from relevant information that contradicts the presenter's assertions, and because they are based on the belief that attacking the source of an argument amounts to refuting the argument. There are several different kinds of ad hominem arguments aspiring critical thinkers should be familiar with including the following: qualifications argument, false motives argument, poisoning-the-well argument, hypocrisy argument, connections argument, do-not-criticize argument, and tone-of-voice argument.
- In today's culture, critical thinkers are going to be subjected to ad hominem attacks. Count on it. Consequently, it is important for aspiring critical thinkers to know how to respond to these attacks. Effective methods for doing so include the following: challenge the attack directly, explain the attack is irrelevant, and brush off the attack as irrelevant.

11

DO NOT GIVE IN TO THE CANCEL CULTURE

*C*ancel culture is a method of trying to silence or invalidate someone who holds beliefs different than the canceler. It is an outgrowth of political correctness that has evolved into a mob mentality. Canceling someone violates the individual's First Amendment rights. There are different forms of cancellation including the following: censorship of speech, rewriting of history, false accusations intended to hurt someone, silencing points of view one disagrees with, boycotting businesses, getting people fired from their jobs, and attacking cultural traditions.

The cancel culture has a dampening effect on free speech and public discourse. It is a counter-productive movement that fails to solve problems, does nothing to encourage positive social change, encourages intolerance and bullying, shuts down open and intelligent dialogue on issues, and creates an environment of fear and bottled-up anger. This is why it is important for critical thinkers to stand up to the cancel culture. Silence can be interpreted as approval.

In today's woke culture, people who express conservative views, speak out in favor of traditional American values, or seek the truth are likely to be targets of the cancel culture mob. The cancel culture has nothing to do with truth, but is based in deception, distortion, and lies. For this reason, some critical thinkers—people who seek the truth—are afraid to speak out. They fear being attacked and canceled. This is a mistake. When we fail to stand up to the cancel culture, the "I think, I feel, and I want" crowd wins and truth loses.

Advocates of the cancel culture claim it is intended to hold people accountable for their views. Opponents counter the cancel culture's real intent is to censor views differing from those of the canceler. The accountability argument would have more validity if the cancel culture focused on holding *all* people accountable instead of focusing on conservatives who hold to traditional American values. But even then, there is a problem. Who decides what is acceptable and what is not?

CRITICISMS OF THE CANCEL CULTURE

The cancel culture may have started out as an attempt to hold people accountable for their words and actions. For example, censoring the words terrorists post online. If this contention was ever true, it is no longer. The cancel culture has become a way for Leftist ideologues to destroy people with opposing views. Criticism of the cancel culture includes the following:

- People use it to try to boost their egos at the expense of others.
- Often, those who are canceled are people who hold conservative views and respect traditional American values.
- The attacks are typically false and made up to destroy anyone who disagrees with a certain point of view.
- Censorship violates the First Amendment right to free speech.

- Canceling people just makes matters worse by creating an angry backlash.
- The threat of cancellation is an attempt to force a certain point of view on others.
- The cancel culture is based on making people afraid to express their views.
- The cancel culture tries to shame and destroy people rather than holding them accountable.
- The cancel culture creates animosity and an us-versus-them mentality, leading people to take sides and attack each other.
- Canceling people can cause them to suffer anxiety, depression, and even PTSD. They can feel lonely, isolated, and rejected.
- The cancel culture has more to do with virtue signaling than accountability.
- Canceling someone is an act of insecurity done because the canceler cannot defend his point of view with logic, reason, or facts.

EXAMPLES OF THE CANCEL CULTURE

There are many well-known examples of the egregious actions of cancel culture advocates and a lot more lesser-known examples. In this section, we summarize some of both. The actions of cancel culture advocates include such things as boycotting businesses, canceling access to online communications, attempting to have people fired from their jobs, and smearing the character of those with opposing voices. The goal of the cancel culture is fear. They want to spread the message that if you oppose their views, you will pay a price. Here are some examples—some well-known and some not—illustrating how vicious and punitive the cancel culture can be.

- ***Donald Trump.*** The censoring of Donald Trump by Twitter is probably the best known and certainly one of the most egregious examples of the cancel culture. Granted, Donald Trump has a caustic personality, but he was president of the United States when Twitter canceled his account, not a terrorist. Twitter claimed the president's messages on their platform violated the company's Glorification of Violence policy. In fact, the president simply called the people who stormed the Capitol on January 6 "patriots." People on different sides of the issue will, of course, see it differently but an honest person would have to admit his words were political speech, not an appeal to violence. Twitter also banned the accounts of two Trump supporters: Michael Flynn, former national security advisor and Sidney Powell, an attorney close to Trump.

- *Aunt Jemima and Mrs. Butterworth's.* These two long-time food brands were canceled because Leftist ideologues claimed they perpetuated stereotypes. Aunt Jemima was the brand for a popular pancake mix and Mrs. Butterworth's was the brand for a best-selling syrup. Aunt Jemima is black. Apparently to some, a black woman making pancakes is offensive. As a result of these cancellations, businesses nationwide are scrambling to find more politically correct names for their products. In the process, they are spending thousands of dollars and losing business because people do not recognize their new brands.

- *Dr. Seuss.* The publisher of Dr. Seuss books decided to discontinue publication of six of his books. The books of this best-selling children's author have been on the market for years and read without offense. But a small minority on the Left decided six of his books contain racist content. As result, the publisher immediately discontinued them. This wasn't just ill-advised; it was cowardly on the part of the publisher. Parents should decide what books their children are going to read or have read to them, not a small minority of Leftist ideologues pushing a woke agenda.

- **Goya.** Goya is one of the largest Hispanic-owned food brands in America. The CEO of Goya made a speech supporting Donald Trump in 2020 and soon found himself being attacked from the Left. Calls for boycotting Goya soon went viral on social media and were picked up by organizations such as the United Farm Workers and United We Dream. An individual who has climbed the corporate ladder and made his company into a great success should have the right to express his views without being attacked by radical Leftists advancing a politically-correct agenda.
- **Ben Shapiro.** Shapiro has a long record of speaking on college campuses, challenging students to seek the truth and not be guided by feelings or emotions. He is a staunch supporter of Israel including its actions against Palestinians. As a result, he has been boycotted by a long list of colleges and universities. This is clearly a violation of his First Amendment right to free speech, but Leftwing activists care little about free speech except their own. Further, intellectually weak, immature college students cannot bear to hear anything they disagree with. Rather than have to think and consider other points of view, they wrap themselves in their comfortable woke cocoons of ignorance and refuse to listen.
- **Joe Rogan.** Joe Rogan is a UFC commentator, podcaster, actor, and comedian. During the COVID epidemic he was accused of being opposed to vaccinations. He denied the claim but nonetheless was attacked by musicians who encouraged Spotify which carries his podcast to boycott him. Prominent among the musicians who wanted him canceled were Neil Young and Joni Mitchell. Although he denied being anti-vaccination, that was not the point. Regardless his views on vaccination, Joe Rogan has a Constitutional right to speak his mind on the subject and any other subject without being harassed by practitioners of the cancel culture. You do not have freedom of speech until you

can say things people do not like to hear without fear of being canceled.

- **_Chris Harrison._** Chris Harrison hosted the popular television program _The Bachelor_ for twenty seasons before being canceled. His offense in the eyes of cancel culture practitioners? He defended a one-time contestant on _The Bachelor_ who attended an Antebellum party. The cancel culture crowd claimed the Old South party was offensive to minorities because of its celebration of a time when slavery was perpetuated in the South. In canceling Harrison and relieving him of his emcee job, the offended parties were making a mountain out of a mole hill. Some people are determined to be offended and are not happy unless they are.

- **_J. K. Rowling._** Rowling, author of the hugely popular Harry Potter books, was subjected to the wrath of the cancel culture when they accused her of being a bigot because of her stand on the transgender issue. Her view that men are men and women are women is held by most people, but it sparked an avalanche of vitriol from Leftist ideologues who cannot abide opposing views. They would rather destroy an individual than allow her to speak her mind openly, truthfully, and freely. Rather than engage opponents in open and helpful dialogue, they prefer to wrap themselves in their comfortable cocoon of ignorance and intolerance so they do not have to hear opposing views.

FIGHTING BACK AGAINST THE CANCEL CULTURE

When Franklin Delano Roosevelt said, "All we have to fear is fear itself," he could have been talking about how to respond to the despicable actions of the cancel culture. Critical thinkers need not fear the cancel culture. Fear is precisely the goal of cancel culture practitioners. They want to force opponents of their Leftist views to remain silent or face the consequences. The answer to dealing with the cancel culture crowd is to stop the cowardly silence that allows them to intimidate opponents.

In the Marine Corps, we learned the best defense is a strong and overpowering offense. Going on the offensive is how critical thinkers should respond when attacked by Leftwing ideologues bent on destroying them. When you, friends, or trusted colleagues are called vile names by Leftist ideologues, speak up. Defend yourself as well as your friends and colleagues. When you are fired because your company is guilty of corporate cowardice, sue for wrongful termination.

Silence is the friend of the cancel culture crowd. Do not be silent. Counter their false claims with logic, reason, and truth. Defending the truth is never the wrong thing to do. In fact, defending the truth will increase your standing among people who do not know you and have only read what the cancel culture says about you. Truth will triumph over lies, but only if someone has the courage to speak the truth. As a critical thinker, be that person who is willing to speak the truth.

SUMMARY

- The cancel culture is a method of trying to silence or invalidate someone who holds an opposing view. It is an outgrowth of political correctness that has evolved into mob rule and widespread bullying. The goal of the cancel culture crowd is to intimidate opponents by striking fear into their hearts about the possible consequences of expressing their views. Canceling someone violates their First Amendment right to freedom of speech.
- There are different forms of cancellations including the following: censorship of speech, rewriting of history, false accusations intended to smear a person's character, silencing the views of opponents, boycotting businesses, getting

people fired from their jobs, and attacking long-standing
cultural traditions and values.
- Criticism of the cancel culture includes the following:
  - People use it to try to boost their egos at the expense of
    others.
  - Most victims of the cancel culture are conservatives who
    respect traditional American values.
  - Cancel culture attacks are false and intended to destroy
    people with opposing views.
  - Censorship violates the First Amendment.
  - Canceling people often makes matters worse by creating
    an angry backlash.
  - Canceling an individual is an attempt to force a certain
    point of view on others.
  - The cancel culture attempts to make people afraid to
    express their opinions.
  - The cancel culture aims to shame people rather than
    hold them accountable.
  - Canceling people creates an us-against-them mentality
    that leads people to take sides and attack each other.
  - Canceling people can cause them anxiety, depression,
    and even PTSD.
  - The cancel culture has more to do with virtue signaling
    than accountability.
- Canceling someone is an act of insecurity because the canceler cannot defend his point of view with logic, reason, or
  common sense.
- Widely publicized examples of victims of the cancel culture
  include Donald Trump, the Aunt Jemima and Mrs. Butterworth's brands, Dr. Seuss, Goya, Ben Shapiro, Joe
  Rogan, Chris Harrison, and J. K. Rowling. These are just
  a few of the celebrities who have been canceled for holding
  views which Leftist ideologues find offensive. There are
  many other examples including politicians, actors, comics,
  pastors, and people from every field of endeavor.

- Critical thinkers can fight back against the cancel culture by refusing to remain silent. Silence is the best friend of the cancel culture. When seekers of the truth remain silent out of fear of being canceled themselves, a small minority of Leftist ideologues wins and truth loses. Truth will win out in the end if critical thinkers have the courage to speak it. When fighting back against the cancel culture, the best defense is a strong offense.

12

RECOGNIZE AND REJECT OVERSIMPLIFICATION

*W*e all like things to be simple. Complex, overly detailed explanations can cause people to tune out or throw up their hands in frustration over trying to understand. The "I think, I need, and I want" crowd knows this and attempts to use it to their advantage when pushing an agenda or trying to gain approval of a weak argument. Those who give into oversimplification are being intellectually lazy; something critical thinkers cannot afford to do.

To understand oversimplification, one must first understand the concept of flaws. A flaw in an argument is an assertion based on insufficient information, deception, distortion, or outright lying. Oversimplification is a false argument because it relies on flawed information to advance an agenda or support an assertion. Oversimplification amounts to purposely minimizing causal factors that might be relevant to the argument. The purpose of an honest discussion is to enhance understanding, not to deceive the audience. Hence, oversimplification is a flawed concept.

There is a principle known as Occam's Razor in which it is claimed the simplest explanation is the best explanation. The title of the concept comes from a misspelling of William of Ockham's name. He was a medieval philosopher and theologian. The problem with the concept, as any critical thinker will see immediately, is the simplest explanation is not necessarily the best. It might be, and certainly deserves due attention to make that determination, but not all issues can be pared down to a simple one- or two-factor explanation. Some issues are complex and nuanced.

EXAMPLES OF OVERSIMPLIFICATION

In this section we examine several examples of oversimplification and demonstrate why the simplest explanation may not be the right explanation. Consider this example. Assume there was another mass shooting at a school. A student from the school was the shooter. People interviewed about the shooter claim she grew up playing with guns, which explains why she shot up the school. This is an oversimplification of what could be a complex situation.

The fact the shooter grew up playing with guns accounts for the fact she knew how to use one, but it does not explain why she made the choice to use it in a violent way. Questions that might be asked by critical thinkers include: Was she angry at the school for some reason? Did she have a grudge against a teacher, administrator, counselor, or student? Was she suffering from mental illness? Did she want to see her name in the newspaper and on the nightly news? There are a lot of factors that might have a bearing on why she chose to engage in such violence, and they deserve due consideration.

Consider another example. So many young people turn to suicide these days because of pressure they feel from social media. While it is true that pressure from social media might contribute to the suicide problem in America, it is also true there may be other factors. Questions critical thinkers might ask include the following: What was the suicide victim's home life like? Did he have supportive parents? Did he have someone in his life he could talk to when feeling depressed? Had there been a major event in his life that left him heartbroken, angry, or resentful? Although social media pressure can be a causal factor in teen suicides, the issue is probably more complicated than this one factor.

The woke policies adopted by many colleges and universities are the result of hippies from the 1960s and '70s becoming tenured professors and taking over our institutions of higher education and using their positions to advocate for Marxism. This is an example that makes an important point about recognizing and rejecting overly simplified arguments. The causal factor claimed is in fact true, but is Leftist ideologues taking over colleges and universities the only factor? Probably not.

Much has changed in American culture contributing to the Marxist tyranny now dominating campus life. Marxist professors could not have the influence they have gained unless they had a willing audience they could turn into a constituency. Here is where they got that willing audience. Before they matriculated at their college or university, college students spent twelve years in public school learning to hate America and reject any view that did not agree with that line of thinking. As a result, many indoctrinated college students are now intellectual midgets who would rather wrap themselves up in their safe spaces of intolerance than learn from a differing point of view.

There is a movement afoot in our country to remove Asian Americans from the list of minorities. Why? Because they are typically so successful in school and in their chosen professions. This is one of the most absurd oversimplifications the Left could possibly devise. Think about what this claim means. For one thing it means being a minority no longer has to do with race or percentage of population but is now based on how successful a racial group is. It is insulting to black and Hispanic Americans because it tells them they are designated minority groups because they cannot succeed. This assertion flies in the face of the fact that some of the most successful people in this country are black and Hispanic Americans. Finally, it overlooks the fact Asian Americans tend to be studious in school, and they work harder and smarter in their careers.

A final example of oversimplification is the high school football coach who gathers his team and shouts, "We are losing every game because you don't want to win!" A critical thinker would immediately recognize this as oversimplification. Who says the players do not want to win? What other reasons might there be for the team's losing streak? Is the coach playing the right players at the right positions? Are any of the team's key players injured and unable to play? Is the coach studying opponents before developing a game plan? The list of causal factors in this case could go on and on.

WHY DO PEOPLE OVERSIMPLIFY?

People who resort to oversimplification to validate their assertions and proposals do so because they have an agenda, and getting into the details puts the validity of their agenda at risk. They try to influence people by applying the maxim, "Keep it simple, stupid." The problem they face, though, is critical thinkers are not stupid. In fact, they are quite adept at ferreting out details that have bearing on the discussion in question. Like various other strategies of the "I think, I need, and I want" crowd—strategies such as biased arguments, false motives, pretending opinions are facts, rationalizations, ad hominem arguments, and all the rest—oversimplification is nothing more than another false argument.

FALSE ARGUMENTS USED IN CONJUNCTION WITH OVERSIMPLIFICATION

Those who use oversimplification to falsely convince an audience of their assertions also use other false arguments, often at the same time. Aspiring critical thinkers should be aware of this approach. What follows are the arguments the "I think, I need, and I want" crowd often introduce along with oversimplification.

QUESTIONABLE-CAUSE ARGUMENT

This argument posits a correlation is the same thing as causation. This is a false argument. One cannot accurately claim a cause-and-effect relationship between factors based on a correlation between them. Because two factors correlate does not mean one causes the other. Correlation is a relationship between two factors. Causation means a change in one factor leads to a change in another factor. A correlation between factors can be observed, but causation is more difficult to determine.

How do non-critical thinkers trying to advance an agenda use the questionable-cause argument in conjunction with oversimplification? Having eliminated relevant facts to simplify their assertions, non-critical thinkers try to claim a correlation between their overly simplified facts amounts to causation, thereby making a false argument leading to a false conclusion.

An example of the questionable-cause argument is children who watch a lot of television or who play a lot of computer games are more violent. Therefore, television and computer games make children more violent. This a questionable-cause argument because, although computer games and television probably are contributing causes, there are other factors that can cause children to become violent. While there may certainly be a correlation between violence in children and television or computer games, or both, a causal relationship would require more study.

SLIPPERY-SLOPE ARGUMENT

The slippery-slope argument is an attempt to prevent someone from making a certain decision or taking a certain action because it will lead to a chain of ever-worsening events. For example, someone might posit that if the government fails to take guns away from all Americans, violent crime will increase, police will not be able to control violence, our cities will be ruled by criminal mobs, and society will break down.

How do non-critical thinkers use the slippery slope argument in conjunction with oversimplification? Having pared their argument down to a few simple facts, they then claim if their conclusion is rejected it will start a chain of events leading to negative or even disastrous consequences. This is a false argument leading to a false conclusion.

The obvious problem with this slippery-slope argument is there are numerous factors causing criminal behavior and no one has shown that removing guns from all Americans—an impossible task—will reduce crime. In fact, it could increase crime. Consequently, the slippery-slope argument is invalid. When presented with a slippery-slope argument, examine the chain of events posited. Is it true that taking the action in question would really cause the chain of negative events to occur? Is there evidence to support this conclusion? Are there other causal factors that should be considered?

FALSE-DILEMMA ARGUMENT

The false-dilemma argument presents two mutually exclusive options as the only options available while avoiding mention of other options. Consider this example. Two parents are discussing where to go on vacation. The husband wants to go to Disneyworld while the wife wants to discuss other options. To bolster his case, the husband uses the false-dilemma argument claiming "if we don't go to Disney World, we will have to go to Sea World and we've been there a hundred times already." This is a false dilemma because there are numerous other vacation venues in the Orlando area and elsewhere in Florida. If the wife accepts this false argument, the family might miss out on something new they would all enjoy.

BEGGING-THE-QUESTION ARGUMENT

The begging-the-question argument assumes the conclusion is correct without any proof or support. For example, assume a company is going to replace its fleet of company cars. A member of the procurement team is trying to convince the procurement officer that Fords are superior to Chevrolets. He has already presented an oversimplified argument about Fords versus Chevrolets. Now he stoops to using the begging-the-question argument by claiming, "Fords are more dependable and last longer. My neighbor drove a Ford for 150,000 miles before trading it in." What you have now is an unsupported argument piled on top of an oversimplified argument.

RED HERRING ARGUMENT

With oversimplification, relevant information is excluded or glossed over because it argues against the presenter's assertions. With the red herring argument, irrelevant information is introduced to distract listeners from the facts left out of the oversimplified argument. It is called the red herring argument because herring give off a strong fishy smell during the curing process. Hence, there is something fishy about this kind of argument.

The way non-critical thinkers use the red herring argument is introducing irrelevant information on top of the oversimplified argument to distract listeners from the flimsiness of the original argument. For example, assume a group of single mothers at work approached the Human Resources Department with a proposal to work from home three days a week. The company's human resources director is against the proposal. She has already presented an oversimplified argument that did not impress the single mothers. To bolster her case, the HR director resorted to using the red herring argument. She claimed, "I won't approve working from home three days a week, but we do offer great benefits." Offering the best benefits in the world does not solve the dilemma these single mothers face. Consequently, this is a red herring argument.

APPEAL-TO-AUTHORITY ARGUMENT

With this false argument, the presenter—seeing his oversimplification strategy is not working—attempts to appeal to authority. He might claim, "The boss likes my idea," or "academic journals support my proposal," when, in fact, neither of these assertions is true. The hope of the presenter is appealing to authority will sway opponents even if they still do not agree with his assertions.

STRAW MAN ARGUMENT

Recall how the straw man argument involves introducing a scenario different from the one an opponent has raised and, then, attacking that false argument. The straw man is the false argument introduced to distract from the oversimplified argument being challenged or even refuted. For example, a presenter's assertion that the sociology department at the local university should institute a new policy requiring students to read a selected list of politically correct books. When a fellow faculty member challenges his proposal, the presenter immediately employs the straw man strategy. He claims, "Do we want to be like the Nazis and burn books?" This is his straw man that he, then, attacks although it has no relevance to the issue in question. Nobody is proposing burning books.

AD HOMINEM ARGUMENT

Recall the ad hominem argument involves attacking an opponent rather than her assertions. The point of the ad hominem argument is to frighten or bully an opponent into going along with the proposal. It is often a strategy of last resort coupled with oversimplification as a Hail Mary strategy when a simplistic argument is clearly failing. For example, assume the presenter claims, "My proposal is simple. It will improve profits, and who can argue against that?" When several listeners want more details about how his proposal will improve profits, the presenter resorts to the ad hominem argument. "What is wrong with you people. I've never met anybody who is against profits." Nobody in the room is against profits, but they would like to see factual evidence that his proposal will enhance the company's profits and not just his personal profits.

A FINAL WORD ON REJECTING THE OVERSIMPLIFICATION ARGUMENT

Non-critical thinkers can be persuasive using such strategies as the oversimplification argument. This is especially the case if they are confident, articulate speakers accustomed to presenting proposals or defending assertions. The oversimplification argument can be an enticing strategy for them because we all like things to be simple and easy to understand. For this reason, it is important for aspiring critical thinkers to be able to recognize and reject the oversimplification argument and any other false arguments non-critical thinkers might use to bolster a weak argument.

The case of a woman we will call Marla Covington is an example of how critical thinkers can handle a persuasive, articulate presenter who uses the oversimplification strategy bolstered by the red herring argument. Marla is a hotel and motel executive whose job involves purchasing hotels, motels, inns, and bed-and-breakfasts, renovating them, and turning them into profit-making ventures. The owner of an older inn in the Catskill Mountains is trying to persuade Marla to purchase his inn. He is using the oversimplification argument, but Marla's not buying it. She has been around the block too many times to be pulled in by a suave speaker with a weak argument.

When the owner finishes his presentation, Marla speaks up. "The approach you have chosen for selling your inn is called the oversimplification argument. You have left out several important details not just relevant to the sale, but critical. For example, you have said nothing about the condition of the facility. If we purchase the inn, will we need to put a new roof on it, update the plumbing, and replace the air conditioning and heating system? Are there other major repairs that will be needed?"

Clearly, taken aback by her frank comments, the owner decided to introduce a red herring argument to draw attention away from repairs needed to the inn. He tells Marla and her team members "We have access to the best ski slopes in the Catskills and the best hiking trails anywhere." Marla responds, "Thanks for that information, ski slopes and hiking trails are an important part of your inn's attraction, but frankly, discussion of ski slopes and hiking trails is a red herring argument. It just diverts us from the real issue which is necessary repairs and renovation."

Marla's approach to dealing with a deceptive presenter is a good one. There is nothing to be gained by beating around the bush with someone who is trying to deceive you. When a presenter realizes you know what he is doing, he will stop doing it which is exactly what critical thinkers want to happen. It is a good way to get to the truth.

SUMMARY

- Oversimplification amounts to paring an argument down to a few supportive facts while leaving out relevant facts that might refute the presenter's conclusion. Of the various false arguments presented in this book, oversimplification is probably the most dangerous because it is so enticing. We all like things to be simple and easy to understand. Consequently, when someone presents a simple and easy-to-understand argument, we are prone to accept it. Therefore, it is critical for aspiring critical thinkers to learn to recognize and reject oversimplification. People oversimplify because there are relevant details they do not want to surface during their proposals. These relevant details might invalidate their argument, so they must be ignored. In addition to oversimplifying arguments, non-critical thinkers will sometimes resort to introducing additional false arguments to draw attention away from their lack of details. These arguments include the following: questionable-cause, slippery slope, false dilemma, begging the question, red herring, appeal to authority, and straw man arguments.

- An example of oversimplification can be seen in the issue of teen suicide. It is often claimed teenagers turn to suicide because they get caught up in social media pressures. This is an overly simplified argument. While it is probably true social media pressures contribute to teen suicide, it is also true that there are numerous other factors that might be causal. The victim's home life, his relationship with his parents, depression, mental-illness, and other factors should also be considered.

13

RECOGNIZE WHEN PEOPLE AVOID INCONVENIENT TRUTHS AND UNCOMFORTABLE FACTS

*A*voiding inconvenient truths and uncomfortable facts is the stock and trade of non-critical thinkers pushing a questionable agenda or debatable assertions. They employ this strategy because certain truths and facts undermine their already false assumptions making them inconvenient and uncomfortable. Any fact or statement of truth that does not fit the mold of their false assertions or weak arguments is considered either inconvenient or uncomfortable.

This avoidance strategy is used as part of several of the false arguments explained in this book including distinguishing between explanations and rationalizations, distinguishing between real solutions and short-term expedients, separating facts from opinions, ad hominem arguments, and recognizing distorted conclusions. The avoidance strategy is often a product of the heart-versus-head dilemma in which individuals must decide to choose between what they feel versus what they know to be true.

Good critical thinkers must be able to think rationally about what they hear, read, and observe and about what they should believe or not believe. They separate facts and truths from opinions and hidden agendas. To review, a fact is a proven truth while an opinion is a statement of personal preference. Separating facts from opinions is important because opinions can be inaccurate, misleading, and unreliable. For example, during a discussion about where to have lunch, one of your colleagues says, "Let's get a pizza. Pizza is good for you." This is obviously an opinion (or perhaps a joke). It would be difficult to recommend pizza as a health food. Let's look at some examples of opinions and facts.

Examples of facts include: there are fifty states in the United States, there are sixty seconds in a minute, the sun rises in the east and sets in the west, human beings require oxygen to stay alive, and some people prefer cats to dogs as pets. Examples of opinions include: our product is the best on the market, this is really a good book, burgers and fries are good for you, he is the best coach in the NFL, and John should have won the tennis match because he is a much better player than Andrew.

WHY PEOPLE AVOID UNCOMFORTABLE FACTS AND INCONVENIENT TRUTHS

You already know why non-critical thinkers and members of the "I think, I need, and I want" crowd avoid uncomfortable facts and inconvenient truths. Facts and truths undermine their already weak arguments. But the issue of avoidance is bigger than just people trying to advance an agenda or score points for their side of an argument. A lot of right-minded, honest people also avoid uncomfortable facts and inconvenient truths.

Aspiring critical thinkers need to understand the concept of avoidance because people who should speak out against a weak argument by an unscrupulous presenter may engage in avoidance when they should speak up. As a critical thinker, you might find yourself in the position of needing to encourage other critical thinkers to stop avoiding and speak up.

Avoidance is often viewed as a heart-versus-head conflict. We know in our heads what is right but our hearts tell us to avoid the truth for reasons of emotion. When we give in to avoidance, we are willingly remaining ignorant when we should be seeking the truth. Consider the following example: National election campaigns are in full swing and the primary vote is looming. Instead of doing deep research on the candidates, you decide to cast your vote for the one running the most TV ads and who seems determined to make positive change. Unfortunately, after the election you discover your choice is just another politician who used deception and obfuscation to win.

For people who are prone to avoidance, emotions trump facts almost every time. They avoid facts and truths that might cause them to re-think what they are doing or saying. They tend to operate according to emotional instincts rather than reason or logic. They look for information that affirms their emotions rather than information that might invalidate them. To understand how powerful emotions can be on an individual's decisions, consider an example from medicine. An individual is having constant pain in his stomach region but refuses to go to the doctor for a checkup because he is afraid it might be cancer.

As an aspiring critical thinker, learn to pay attention not just to presenters who are trying to advance an agenda or convince others of their weak assertions. Also pay attention to listeners who might know the truth but are afraid to speak up because of avoidance. Do not let good people ignore bad arguments because they do not want to hurt someone's feelings or for other emotional reasons.

REVIEW OF HOW TO DISTINGUISH FACTS VERSUS OPINIONS

You learned in chapter 8 how to separate facts from opinions. This is a challenge you will face when dealing with people who avoid uncomfortable facts and inconvenient truths. What can you base your decision on when trying to distinguish between facts and opinions? There are a number of criteria to be familiar with. For example, an individual can base his statements on research or personal preference. Is the statement objective or subjective? Is what being said even possible? Is the statement presented using biased words? Is it debatable? Does the statement represent something that actually happened? Using criteria such as these you can easily distinguish between fact and fiction, and recognize when someone is avoiding uncomfortable facts and inconvenient truths.

Before proceeding, we review the differences between facts and truths versus opinions and feelings. Remember the following differences when evaluating what you hear, read, or observe:

- Facts can be proven true; opinions cannot.
- Facts are objective; opinions are subjective.
- Facts are not debatable, opinions are.
- Facts are more likely to lead to the truth; opinions based on feelings or incomplete information because of avoidance lead to bad decisions.
- Facts can be presented with unbiased words; opinions are based on bias.
- Facts are the same for different people; they are universal. Opinions vary from person to person.
- Facts are supported by research; opinions are proven faulty by research.

Let's contrast two people: one a critical thinker and the other an avoidance-oriented individual. Micah tests everything he hears, reads, or observes. He asks such questions as "Can that opinion be tested through research, is it debatable, is it presented in unbiased terms, is it universal or can it change from person to person?" By applying these kinds of questions, Micah is good at sorting out facts from fiction and recognizing when someone is avoiding inconvenient truths and uncomfortable facts.

One day Micah was debating a fellow college student outside class. The debate centered around the efficacy of the government forgiving student loans. Micah, who is working his way through college, is opposed to loan forgiveness while his fellow student, Angela, supports the concept. Angela claims forgiving student loans is a good idea because it will make college graduates better citizens. Micah asked his usual questions about this claim and came to the obvious conclusion that Angela was way off the mark in her opinion. She was avoiding some uncomfortable facts and inconvenient truths about student loans.

He told Angela a few things that could be verified by research such as student loan forgiveness can create an entitlement mentality in college graduates. It can also add immeasurably to the national debt putting America's future at risk. His final statement was it is unfair to expect Americans who never went to college to pick up the tab for those who did.

Micah's points were accurate, logical, and reasonable. Yet Angela still clung to her opinion as fact. She, like so many of her fellow students, was buried in student debt she irresponsibly borrowed to pay for a degree with little or no value in the marketplace. Unable to pay the debt, she wants the government to do it. All Angela can see is what she wants; not what is right or true. Consequently, she is willing to avoid uncomfortable facts and inconvenient truths she knows in her heart of hearts to be accurate, relevant, and true.

Cindy approaches life from what she thinks, feels, and wants. Truth, to her, is anything that supports her opinion on matters; when uncomfortable facts or inconvenient truths intrude, she ignores them; a fact causing her no end of trouble. In discussions at work, Cindy will lie, distort, and deceive to get her way. Even at home, her husband and children cannot trust her opinions because they are so often biased. At work her job security is in question because of her lies. At home her marriage is shaky because of the deception.

Unfortunately, her sense of "I think, I feel, and I want" is too strong for Cindy to break her habit of lying. Just last week at work, Cindy told her boss she completed a project she had not even started. Because of her lie, the project was eventually completed late and Cindy's company lost the contract. That was the last straw for her boss. Cindy was fired an hour after the contract fell through.

Try this exercise. Here is an example of an assertion often made by politicians pushing an agenda: teaching Critical Race Theory (CRT) to school children will make them better citizens. Let's test this assertion.

- Does this assertion represent information testable through research? It does not because the assertion is unprovable. How do we know if one single factor made people better citizens? The only way to know would be to follow up those who were taught CRT over the course of a lifetime and observe how their lives tuned out. Even then, how would you know if the outcome could be attributed to CRT or to other factors? Bottom line? You cannot.
- Is the assertion objective or subjective? The assertion is subjective because there is no proof it accurately represents the truth. Because it is subjective, ten different people might have ten different opinions about its efficacy with no way to pin down the actual truth. Of course, an inability to determine the truth of the assertion makes it a false assertion.
- Is the assertion debatable? It is. Any assertion based on "I think, I need, and I feel" is debatable. A supporter of CRT could certainly try to make a case for teaching the concept to children, but it is a difficult assertion to validate. Further, debate, no matter how eloquent, does not change the truth.
- Is the assertion likely to influence people? Probably not. Even if coherently and articulately presented, the assertion

rests on a foundation of sand. CRT teaches that minorities have been victims of white supremacy forever and always will be. Even prima facie research shows black Americans who are critical thinkers and who believe in the values that have helped other Americans succeed do well in this country. We have had a black president, black vice-president, numerous black members of Congress, as well as successful entrepreneurs, engineers, scientists, professors, and teachers. In fact, black Americans who hold to traditional American values have prospered in every field of endeavor.

- Is the assertion presented with biased words? It invariably is. CRT takes its roots back to slavery in American, something done away with on December 6, 1865, by the 13th Amendment to the U.S. Constitution. Because slavery once existed, it will always exist in one form or another according to CRT advocates. This, of course, is demonstrably false. Another major component of CRT is reparations to descendants of slaves. CRT advocates for people who have never owned slaves to pay monetary reparations to people who have never been slaves. The illogic and unfairness of this demand are easy for critical thinkers to recognize and reject. CRT is a lie and should be treated as one.
- Is the assertion universal? Obviously not. In fact, it is held by a minority of Americans. Different people can have different opinions about teaching CRT to school children, and they do.
- Is the assertion supported by research? No. In fact, research refutes the assertion. Even surface-level research reveals facts contrary to the opinion.

Mike could not believe what he was hearing. He invited his sister Veronica's new fiancé, Joel, to join his family for Easter dinner. Everything went well until he prayed over the meal and asked everyone to go around the table and tell what they were thankful for on the day of Christ's resurrection.

When it was Joel's turn, he said: "I don't pray. It is a useless exercise. You all pray to a God that doesn't even exist."

Mike, taken aback, responded, "No, we pray to a living God who is with us right now in this room in the form of the Holy Spirit." Joel responded, "That may be your truth. But it's not mine." "So, you think truth is a flexible concept that can be decided by individuals depending on what they think, feel, or want." Joel replied, "Exactly!" "What, then, happens when your truth and my truth conflict? There are millions of people in the world. If they can all have their own truths, we are left with nothing but chaos, conflict, and strife.

"Let me ask you a question, Joel. What is going to happen when you and Veronica are married and she decides that her truth is adultery is acceptable? What happens when someone decides their truth makes killing your children acceptable? You might want to rethink your position on truth." Joel fumbled for answers but could come up with nothing that made sense. After a few minutes of confusion he said, "Thanks for the invitation. I'll be leaving now."

Critical thinkers go where the truth leads them. They do not avoid uncomfortable facts or inconvenient truths discovered along the way. Those facts and those truths get factored into the discussion and they influence the final conclusion. Consequently, it is important for aspiring critical thinkers to learn to recognize when people are avoiding uncomfortable truths and inconvenient facts regardless what side of the argument they are on.

AVOIDING UNCOMFORTABLE FACTS AND INCONVENIENT TRUTHS IN POLITICS

Politicians regularly avoid uncomfortable facts and inconvenient truths. You see it in television and in-person interviews all the time. A politician is asked a difficult question and, rather than answer it, he goes off on a tangent avoiding the uncomfortable facts or inconvenient truths raised by the question. Because they are always pushing an agenda, politicians become adept at avoiding input that does not support their agenda and presenting only information that validates their argument.

One of the reasons politicians and those who support them avoid uncomfortable facts and inconvenient truths is the human need for affiliation—the need to be accepted as part of a group. For these people, belonging to a group such as a political party is more important than the truth. For example, assume a politician is pushing an agenda including raising the debt ceiling and increasing spending at the same time. When challenged on the logic of doing so, the politician—who knows what he is proposing is wrong—sticks to his argument because it is part of his political party's platform. This kind of party loyalty has led politicians who know better to support defunding the police, teaching CRT in elementary schools, and supporting district attorneys who pamper criminals while stepping on the rights of law-abiding citizens.

Choosing party over truth leads to the polarization of society. People listen only to the news programs that confirm their party's beliefs, surround themselves with like-minded friends, and read only those news stories that confirm their preconceived notions. When this happens, as it has in contemporary America, what is lost are facts and the truth.

SUMMARY

- Aspiring critical thinkers need to understand why people avoid uncomfortable facts and inconvenient truths. There is the obvious reason that unscrupulous presenters want to hide any information that does not support their agenda. But this is not the only reason. Honest, right-minded people will sometimes engage in avoidance. They do this when in heart-versus-head debates, the heart wins. Some people—even critical thinkers—will occasionally give in to emotions and, as a result, avoid uncomfortable facts and inconvenient truths.

- Critical thinkers can separate facts from opinions. They can think objectively about what they hear, read, observe, and experience.

- A fact is a proven truth while an opinion is a statement of personal preference.

- Separating facts from opinion is important because opinions can be inaccurate, misleading, and unreliable.

- Differences between facts and opinions include facts can be proven while opinions cannot; facts are objective while opinions are subjective; facts are not debatable while opinions are; facts are more likely to influence the decisions of others while opinions have little influence, particularly on critical thinkers; facts can be presented with unbiased language while opinions are based on bias; facts are the same for different people—they are universal—while opinions can vary from person to person; and facts are supportable by research while opinions are proven faulty by research.

- Opinions and assertions can be tested for accuracy and validity by asking the following questions: Is the assertion testable through research? Is the assertion objective or subjective? Is the assertion debatable? Is the assertion likely to influence people? Is the assertion presented using unbiased language? Is the assertion universal? Is the assertion supported by research?

- Politicians and those who support them often avoid uncomfortable facts and inconvenient truths because party loyalty and a sense of belonging are more important to them than the truth.

14

RECOGNIZE AND REJECT DISTORTED CONCLUSIONS

A conclusion is a judgment reached through reason, logic, and a thorough examination of all relevant facts. A valid conclusion is based on truth. A distorted conclusion is one based on faulty or incomplete information. In other words, it is the kind of biased, irrational conclusion unscrupulous presenters try to slip by others who have a stake in the decisions to be made based on the conclusion.

Presenters often make the mistake—intentional or not—of conflating correlation with causation. They are not the same thing. Neither is it accurate to think a coincidence equals causation. You have probably heard someone say, "I don't believe in coincidence." People who believe this or that correlation equals causation are prone to turn unrelated factors into causal factors which, in turn, makes for distorted conclusions.

Let's look at a distorted conclusion and the problems it might have caused. There are more than 1,000 train derailments in the United States every year. One railroad line is prone to derailments, accounting for more than its competing lines. After a particularly bad derailment in which toxic materials polluted the water and air of an entire town, causing evacuations and the hospitalization of local citizens, the management team of the railroad called an internal meeting to investigate the "why" behind its mounting derailments.

One particularly convincing investigator blamed the derailments on the engineers, claiming they had insufficient training to deal with emergencies. He was so convincing that the railroad's management team was ready to accept his conclusion and increase training for engineers believing that would solve the problem. Fortunately, they decided to hear from other investigators from the company's safety department.

The safety department was very specific in their recommendations and supported their assertions with accurate data. They claimed the problem was the result of more than one factor. After assuring the management team they would never argue against training for engineers or any other railroad employee, they made it clear a lack of training was not the cause of the spate of derailments the company was experiencing.

According to the safety investigators, the problem was threefold: First, the braking systems for their trains were outdated and lacking in regular maintenance. Second, individual train cars were being overloaded requiring them to carry more weight than they were rated for, and third, the company's trains were pulling too many cars at a time. All three of these claims were supported by hard, irrefutable facts. As a result, the company's management team accepted the conclusion of the safety investigators. Had the team accepted the distorted conclusion of the first investigator, derailments would have continued and gotten worse.

RECOGNIZING AND REJECTING DISTORTED CONCLUSIONS

A conclusion takes the following form: If we know X, we can conclude Y. Because of this, critical thinkers engaged in discussions of proposals, issues, or assertions ask themselves and their colleagues, "From what we have been told, what can we reasonably conclude?" They know Y can be concluded from X only if X is complete and accurate. Let's consider an example to illustrate this point.

The high school history department is debating updates to how American history should be taught. The debate centers around the question of whether America should be portrayed as a shameful nation because of slavery or an exceptional nation for overcoming the scourge of slavery, making equal opportunity a reality, and saving the world from totalitarianism. Tina Brown is trying to make a case for the contention that America is a nation built by rich white men for rich white men. Gary Stevens responds, "I suppose your contention is why we have had a black president, black vice president, many black and other minority members of Congress, and some of the most successful people in America in all fields of endeavor are minorities. It's obvious your conclusion is distorted by a lack of relevant information." Gary's argument won out because he backed it with irrefutable facts rather than a biased agenda.

The best work done on distorted thinking can be accredited to psychiatrist David Burns. The distortions presented in this section are identified in his book, *Feeling Good Handbook* (1989, Plume Publishing, updated May 1999). But the definitions and examples of distorted thinking are strictly ours.

ALL-OR-NOTHING THINKING

This form of distortion occurs when proponents refuse to acknowledge shades of gray and nuances in arguments. They want their proposals to be accepted in total as perfect. They also tend to view opposing arguments as all bad no matter how much validity they have. Presenters who take this approach want listeners to accept their proposals completely without any alterations. With them, it is all or nothing.

Let's look at an example of this kind of distorted thinking. Andy, an assistant coach, is trying to convince the coaching staff to change its game plan for the upcoming championship game. He wants to increase passing, cut back on the running game, and go to a no-huddle offense. His fellow coaches like the idea of the no-huddle offense, but reject the passing and running recommendations. Andy, an all-or-nothing thinker, stomps out of the locker room in a huff.

MENTAL FILTERING

This form of distortion occurs when proponents focus on a single item of input and exclude all others—filter them out—especially those that do not fit their assertions. Let's consider an example of this kind of thinking. Andrea made an excellent proposal to change certain aspects of her company's marketing plan. Her proposal was well-received except for one item. Andrea went back to her office feeling like a failure because just one of her recommendations was rejected rather than the success it really was. Why? Because the item rejected was the item she was focused on. All the others she blocked out by mental filtering.

JUMPING TO CONCLUSIONS

This form of distortion occurs when proponents of a given proposal think they know what others are thinking. This leads them to draw conclusions based on limited information because they minimize or ignore what they believe others are thinking about their assertions. They avoid relevant data because they think others will oppose it. Let's look at an example of this kind of distortion.

Mikala is trying to convince her editorial team to issue a contract for a manuscript she has received. The manuscript is for a how-to book, and Mikala's company has never published a how-to book. She thinks she knows exactly how the rest of the team will react to a proposal for a how-to book. Consequently, Mikala never uses the term "how-to." It turns out jumping to conclusions was a mistake. The executive editor for her company had been contemplating adding how-to books to their inventory for some time and, for her, the timing was perfect. She told Mikala if she could make the manuscript into a how-to book, the team would issue a contract.

MAGNIFICATION/MINIMIZATION

This form of distortion occurs when proponents exaggerate or minimize the importance of relevant input to bolster their assertions. If a presenter thinks certain items of input will undermine his agenda, he might minimize the importance of those items. If he thinks certain items of input will bolster his agenda, he might magnify the importance of those items of input.

Let's consider an example of this distorted way of thinking. Rupert is trying to convince his fellow coaches to start a different pitcher in the next game. He has an agenda. Rupert's best friend's son, Lonnie, is a second-string pitcher on his team. Rupert promised his friend he would try to convince the coaching staff to elevate Lonnie to the starting rotation. When a fellow coach brings up Lonnie's poor earned run average (ERA), Rupert minimizes this coach's input claiming, "Lonnie is better than his record implies. He just needs more time on the mound."

During the same discussion, Rupert engages in magnifying. Another coach offered his opinion that Lonnie did have a good outing the last time he pitched although it was against a weak team. Seizing on the good outing claim and ignoring the weak team input, Rupert claimed having a good outing demonstrated Lonnie's talent. Because of Rupert's enthusiasm, the coaching staff agreed to let Lonnie start the next game. He was knocked out of the box in the second inning, giving up five runs before being pulled. This is the quintessential example of how magnifying and minimizing can lead to a distorted conclusion.

EMOTIONAL REASONING

This form of distortion occurs when proponents think with their hearts instead of their heads. Emotional reasoning is not really reasoning at all because it tends to cancel out hard facts and relevant data with emotions close to the heart of the presenter. Some people develop an emotional attachment to their arguments and assertions. When this happens, they have a hard time listening to hard facts and relevant information. Consider this example of emotional reasoning.

The procurement department of his company was discussing which airline to contract with for employee travel. Beckham Burns—usually a critical thinker—is emotionally attached to a certain airline because his dad flew for this airline his entire career. Beckham grew up interacting with pilots, stewards, and crew members of the airline. Hence, he has an emotional attachment to what he is proposing.

The problem with his proposal is the airline in question has the worst safety record and worst on-time arrival record of all the airlines being proposed. In addition, it has submitted the highest bid of all the airlines being considered. These are important and relevant facts critical thinkers could not overlook, and it damaged Beckham in the eyes of his colleagues that he could overlook them. His conclusion concerning which airline to choose was obviously distorted by emotion.

PERSONALIZATION

This form of distortion occurs when proponents of a given point of view or proposal take challenges personally and react negatively as a result. No matter what the challenge may be, they are offended by it. Often, they react by lashing out at those who challenge their assertions using ad hominem attacks or the pity strategy. You know all about ad hominem attacks, but what is the pity strategy? The following example demonstrates this infrequently used, but still important form of distorted thinking.

Miranda's presentation was not going well. Her colleagues—all men—were not buying what she was trying to sell. Unable to back up her proposal with hard facts, logic, or reasoning Miranda gave up and told the group, "You are rejecting my proposal because I am a woman. If one of you men made the same proposal, it would be accepted unanimously." Having said this, Miranda stomped out of the room in a huff.

CONTROL FALLACY

This form of distortion occurs when proponents of an agenda think they are in complete control of events, including the thinking of other stakeholders in the discussion. This is a dangerous distortion because it can lead to animosity when it becomes obvious those who think they are in control are not. They can quickly adopt an attitude that says. "Who do you think you are opposing me?" Consider the following example of the control fantasy.

When his company was a small business, Morgan Tuttle controlled everything from production, to marketing, to inventory, and human resources. He liked being in control. When he decided on something, his decision was law. No one dared oppose him because he controlled everything including their job security. However, all of this changed when he took his company public. He now had to contend with a board of directors who represented stockholders. This was new territory for Morgan, and he did not like it. After the board of directors challenged several of his proposals, Morgan became so angered at his loss of control he decided to sell the business.

FAIRNESS FALLACY

This form of distortion occurs when proponents expect everything to be fair in a rarely fair world. Critical thinkers know the world is not fair. They do everything they can to make it so, but understand life is not always going to be fair. When a presenter thinks it is unfair his proposal is not winning the support hoped for, his response is often anger, resentment, or frustration, or even hopelessness. These emotions may prevent him from offering other ideas he has for improvements in the future; ideas that might have validity. Consider the following example of how the fairness fallacy can undermine the continual improvement process.

Heather Muldroon wanted life to be fair. She tried to be fair to others and expected them to be fair with her. As a result, she was often disappointed. She worked hard on a proposal to improve the reading skills of children at the elementary school where she taught. Only 20 percent of fourth graders at her school could read at grade level. Her idea was to go back to teaching phonics instead of continuing the obvious failure of the "see-and-say" method now in use.

Unfortunately, her colleagues were graduates of watered-down educational programs that taught them to use the "see-and-say" method, and not even one of them wanted to change. Heather thought it unfair that no one agreed with her proposal despite the research she produced in favor of phonics. She responded by becoming resentful and refusing to participate in other meetings about improving the poor performance of students in her school.

ALWAYS-RIGHT FALLACY

This form of distortion occurs when a proponent thinks he is always right and needs to always be right. Anything less is detrimental to his ego. Being wrong is unacceptable, causing presenters to go to any length to prove themselves right. Presenters who must always be right are often unable to disagree without being disagreeable. Critical thinkers need to be well tuned-in when they recognize an I-must-always-be-right attitude in presenters; they will try every trick covered in this book to be right including deception, distortion, and lying. Consider the following example of an individual with an I-must-always-be-right attitude.

Maggie King always had to be right whether in the office or at home. It hurt her in both places. Recently, at home, she and her husband had an argument over what to do about supper. Earlier in the day, Maggie called her husband and left a message that they should eat out that night at a favorite restaurant. When she got home from work that evening, Maggie was too tired to go out, so she begged off eating at their favorite restaurant. Her husband, who had already made reservations was not pleased and told her, "Eating out was your idea not mine. Now you don't want to do it."

Maggie, as was her way, denied eating out was her idea. She made obviously false statements trying to convince her husband it was his idea. She distorted, deceived, and lied. Finally, her husband pulled out his cell phone and played the message she left earlier. Unable to admit to being wrong, Maggie stomped out of the room and locked herself in their bedroom. Her husband, in the meantime, went to their favorite restaurant and ate alone. While eating, he contemplated how much longer he could stay in a marriage with a woman who could not admit to being wrong.

RECOGNIZING AND REJECTING DISTORTED CONCLUSIONS

The first rule in recognizing distorted conclusions is to do your research on the topic in question before entering discussions about it. Those who present distorted conclusions bank on their listeners being uninformed. In this way they can slip biased information pass them while ignoring uncomfortable facts and inconvenient truths.

Once you have done your research, ask yourself the following kinds of questions about what you are being told. Does the input you are receiving comport with what you learned from researching the topic? Does the presenter seem to be emotionally attached to his assertions or agenda? Is the presenter resorting to any of the fallacies explained in this chapter? Do you sense bias in the presenter's arguments? What does common sense tell you about the proposal?

Ask these kinds of questions and you will recognize distorted conclusions which, in turn, will ensure better decisions. Better decisions will, in turn, ensure better quality, productivity, efficiency, effectiveness, and morale.

SUMMARY

- A conclusion is a judgment reached through logic, reason, common sense, and a thorough examination of all relevant facts. A valid conclusion is based on truth. A distorted conclusion is based on faulty, biased, or incomplete information. Proponents of a given agenda sometimes mistake correlation with causation. They are not the same thing. Further, coincidence is not causation.

- A conclusion takes the following form: If we know X, we can conclude Y. This is why it is important for critical thinkers to engaged in discussions to ask themselves and their colleagues, "From what we have been told, what can we reasonably conclude?" Otherwise, you are likely to end up with a distorted conclusion. Distorted thinking leads to distorted conclusions, which, in turn, lead to poor decisions and inadvisable actions. What follows are the most common forms of distorted thinking. It is important for aspiring critical thinkers to learn to recognize and reject these various forms of distorted thinking.

- All-or-nothing thinking occurs when proponents refuse to acknowledge shades of gray and nuances in arguments. Mental filtering occurs when proponents of a given proposal or point of view focus on one item of input to the exclusion of all others. They mentally filter out other items of input. Jumping to conclusions occurs when proponents of a given proposal or point of view believe they know what opponents are thinking and respond by minimizing or ignoring unwanted information they feel might be introduced into the discussion.

- Magnification and minimization are two opposite forms of the same kind of distorted thinking. Magnification occurs when proponents exaggerate the importance of the data they are presenting. Minimization occurs when proponents minimize any input that might undermine their case. Emotional reasoning is a form of distorted thinking when proponents think with their hearts instead of their heads. They become emotionally attached to their proposals or assertions and cancel out any relevant facts running counter to their emotional attachments.

- Personalization occurs when proponents of a given agenda or points of view take challenges to their assertions personally and react negatively as a result. The control fallacy occurs when proponents of a given agenda or point of view believe they oversee the proceedings, only to find out they are not in control. When they see they are going to be challenged, personalization proponents often react in anger, frustration, or resentment. The fairness fantasy occurs when proponents of a given agenda believe they are being treated unfairly by those who challenge them. They want the world to be fair, which it seldom is, and they interpret fairness as agreeing with them. The always-right fallacy occurs when proponents are unable to accept any form of challenge. They must be right in everything all the time. As a result, they resent challenges to their assertions.

- The first rule in recognizing and rejecting distorted thinking and the resultant distorted conclusions is to do your research on the topic in question before entering discussions about it. Once you have done your research, observe how the information presented comports with what you have learned. Are there distortions, generalizations, or speculations in the input you are receiving? Does the presenter seem biased or emotionally attached to his proposal? Do all the parts of her proposal fit together to form a comprehensive, valid argument or are there missing pieces of relevant information? Do you recognize any of the forms of distorted thinking presented herein?

- Aspiring critical thinkers can overcome their reluctance to engage by applying several strategies. You can overcome negative anticipation and fear of consequences by asking yourself, "What is the worst that can happen?" Having asked this question, you remember the things we worry about seldom happen but when they do, are not usually as bad as we thought they would be. Overcoming the fear of a loss of control is a simple matter of telling yourself you are not in control in the first place. In meetings where you apply your critical thinking skills and speak up, you do not have to control the situation. In fact, you cannot. Instead, offer your feedback objectively, tactfully, humbly, and respectfully and you will be able to avoid the need to control the meeting.

- Overcoming the fear of speaking in public can take time so do not rush it. Give it the time it needs. Strategies for overcoming the fear of public speaking include the following: do your research; know the topic in question well; practice what you might say in the meeting; take a couple of deep breaths before speaking; and get comfortable with silence—do not try to fill in the void for presenters. In addition, you can reduce negative consequences of thinking objectively by practicing critical thinking frequently and being humble, respectful, and tactful.

15

LEARN HOW TO ARGUE PRODUCTIVELY

The term *argument* suggests shouting matches in which people attack each other verbally and, sometimes, physically. The resulting resentment and bitterness can ruin a relationship. This is why most people try to avoid arguments. But strife is not what arguments are supposed to be about. Rather, an argument is supposed to be a discussion in which people try to better understand each other and their differing points of view. You may have heard the maxim, "steel sharpens steel." This is what should happen in productive arguments. My assertions should sharpen your argument and yours should sharpen mine.

Arguing productively is a critical thinking skill. If you can participate in discussions in ways that sharpen the presenter's argument, as well as your own, you are arguing productively. Trying to see things through the other person's eyes is always a helpful strategy in discussions of points of view, assertions, and proposals. This does not relieve you of the responsibility for pointing out holes in a proposal or problems with the presenter's assertions. But it does require you to do this in a humble, respectful, tactful, and helpful way. There are several specific strategies for arguing productively that should be part of a critical thinker's toolbox. We explain these strategies in this chapter.

STRATEGIES FOR ARGUING PRODUCTIVELY

The following strategies will help you argue productively without incurring bitterness, resentment, and strife. Learning to apply these strategies effectively takes time and practice. Give them the time they need to sink in and practice, practice, practice. The better you get at arguing productively, the better will be the decisions you are involved in and the less strife there will be in discussions.

DO YOUR RESEARCH

This strategy is fundamental to critical thinking. It has been repeated numerous times in this book. Critical thinkers never engage in a discussion without having fully researched the topic in question. They apply the Boy Scout's motto: "Be prepared." As you listen to the presenter's proposal, ask yourself, "Do her words comport with what I have learned about this topic?"

Alejandro Ruiz was well-known in his company and appreciated for his adept arguing over proposals, points of view, and assertions. He was so good at arguing productively the CEO of his company sometimes invited Alejandro to join in meetings of the executive team just to get his perspective. What was Alejandro's secret? Research. Before engaging in any kind of discussion of an issue, he researched the topic so thoroughly that few in the room knew as much about it as he did.

In a discussion about adopting a new kind of metal for the company's main product—food processors—Alejandro's research came in handy. The employee advocating on behalf of the new metal demonstrated its strength, low cost, and ready availability. The new metal looked like a winner to Alejandro's team. It was not. Alejandro's research revealed the metal tended to deteriorate quickly if exposed to certain acidic foods. Since the company could not control the kinds of foods consumers might put in its food processors, the metal's efficacy was undermined and the company was able to avoid a costly mistake.

DO NOT ARGUE ABOUT EVERYTHING

Never argue for the sake of argument. Some issues are not worth the effort. There will be times when it is better to just walk away and avoid an argument. Mona Sutton was not one to walk away from an argument, no matter how frivolous or inconsequential it might be. She argued about everything, a fact that gave her a reputation as a person to avoid.

For example, when a colleague said he really liked the new cell phone service he contracted with, Mona immediately challenged him and began an argument. The argument ended up in anger, bitterness, and resentment. When the dust settled, Mona lost a friend and added to her reputation as a person to avoid.

This is an argument she should have walked away from, but instead she instigated it. It was not worth the effort because it did not really matter what her colleague thought about his cell phone service or what Mona thought about it. Someone might have told Mona, "If you don't like his company, don't use it. You are not going to argue him out of liking his cell phone service."

BE HUMBLE, RESPECTFUL, AND TACTFUL

The goal of a good argument is to increase the understanding of those involved and the proposal they are making. The idea is not to win the argument, but to use it to improve proposals. The best way to make this happen is to be humble, respectful, and tactful in how you challenge someone's assertions. Your tone of voice, attitude, word choice, and even nonverbal cues can all influence how your feedback is received. Humble, respectful, and tactful feedback is helpful.

Mickey Shiver had to learn this lesson the hard way. Whenever he challenged a presenter's assertions, Mickey was aggressive and arrogant. He gave presenters no credit for the work they had done, acted as if he had superior knowledge, and was not above insulting those who disagreed with him. As a result, his boss finally told Mickey he could no longer participate in team discussions. This, in turn, hurt his career. Mickey ended up having to leave the company and find a job with another employer.

Before he left, his boss pulled him aside and told him, "Mickey, you have a lot of potential, but you are your own worst enemy. Your arrogance and aggressiveness in team discussions do more than turn people off, they make you look mean-spirited and unhelpful. Your feedback—which might be good without the bullying tactics—never gets due consideration because of the way you deliver it. You have a job at a new company, but it won't last long unless you learn to be humble, respectful, and tactful in team discussions."

LISTEN MORE, TALK LESS

You learn a lot more from listening than from talking. If you are going to get a better grasp of what the presenter is proposing, listening is the key. It is not uncommon for opponents of an idea or proposal to speak up prematurely. They do not agree with something said, but they have not given the presenter an opportunity to complete his explanation. Had they waited and listened, he might have added information that changed their mind.

Flora Congrand was not a good listener, which hurt her critical thinking. Often, she would interrupt a presenter before she had time to provide a complete explanation. As you might imagine, this did not go over well with presenters. They considered Flora rude and unhelpful. Consequently, this made her unwelcome in team discussions. Thankfully, Flora got some good advice from a colleague who told her, "Flora, you need to learn to wait before you speak. Listen carefully and completely before you speak up. Your feedback will be received better if you will learn this one thing." It was not easy for her, but Flora eventually learned to listen more and talk less. When this happened, she became a valued member of her team during discussions and debates.

RECOGNIZE VERBAL CUNNING

Some people try to win arguments through cunning and deceit. This caution has been repeated often throughout this book. It is one of the main reasons critical thinking is so important. Critical thinkers can see through this kind of ruse. Proponents of an idea may try to distract listeners with irrelevant information or by using ad hominem attacks, red herrings, and other similar tactics. This happened to Ang Chong when he attended a press conference of a political candidate running for the office of U.S. Senator from his state.

Ang asked a question about the out-of-control national debt. The candidate, clearly uncomfortable with the question, tried to distract Ang by offering irrelevant information about how to protect Social Security and Medicare, neither of which were under attack by any politician in the race. The candidate became even more uncomfortable when Ang asked, "How can you claim to protect Social Security and Medicare when your spending plans will bankrupt the federal government?" Unable to respond logically and reasonably, the candidate cut the press conference short and moved on to another venue.

BE BRIEF AND CONCISE

When arguing an issue or stance, get to the point. Do not fall into the trap of loving to hear your own voice. People are more likely to give due consideration to brief, concise, and to-the-point arguments. No one likes to listen to someone babble on, repeating points he has already made several times. Because of the negative influence of technology, people have short attention spans these days. Keep this in mind when you argue over issues and assertions.

Adela Hernandez was especially good at making brief, concise arguments. Before she spoke, Adela thought hard about what she planned to say and how she would say it. Her nickname among fellow college students was "bumper sticker" because she was so concise her arguments would fit on a bumper sticker. This, of course, was an exaggeration, but she clearly could argue concisely. Because of this, her arguments always got a good hearing, even from those who disagreed with her.

COMPROMISE WHEN IT IS ACCEPTABLE

Never compromise to end an argument unless doing so will bring a positive result. There will be times when arguing that proponents and opponents have common ground. They may differ on less important details, but they can agree on substantial issues. In such cases, compromise is acceptable.

Lacy McKnight, a new member of Congress, discovered the value of compromise when arguing with a fellow legislator about Social Security. Her colleague thought the retirement age for receiving Social Security should be moved up to seventy years of age. Lacy thought it should stay the same and budget cuts in other areas should be made to save the system from bankruptcy. After arguing for a while, Lacy realized, though they disagreed on the details, they both wanted to save the Social Security system. Consequently, she proposed a compromise. Lacy's colleague said, "What if I bring the retirement age down to sixty-eight and you make specific recommendations for cutting the budget in other areas." Her fellow legislator agreed. They compromised in a way that brought a positive result.

WORK TO RESOLVE IMPASSES

It is common for an argument to result in an impasse; neither side is willing to abandon their position or compromise. When this happens, you have two options. The first is to agree to disagree, but there is a major problem with choosing this option because of an impasse: if a decision must be made, agreeing to disagree does not apply. Agreeing to disagree in an argument means you do not resolve the debate and, as a result, no decision is made. The second option is to work behind the scenes to resolve the impasse.

Pete Garcia was good at resolving impasses in arguments. After a meeting of the student council was dismissed because of an impasse, Pete, who was a counselor for the council, did what he often did in these cases. He approached the key proponents and opponents in the debate and asked for a few minutes to discuss the issue.

He would tell proponents and opponents, "Let's look at this issue from another angle." With opponents, he would try to get them to look at the issue through the eyes of proponents and vice-versa. During his discussions he would emphasize the importance of being able to decide and look for common ground between the two sides. He also told them resolving impasses in arguments would be an important tool in their toolbox for success after graduation. Then, he would suggest a compromise if that was appropriate. Often his work brought both sides back to the table and resolved the impasse.

DISAGREE WITHOUT BEING DISAGREEABLE

Being disagreeable—angry, pushy, egotistical, and a know-it-all—shuts down debate and does nothing to contribute to better decisions. There will be times when agreeing to disagree is the only option left to opponents and proponents. When this happens, it is important to disagree without being disagreeable so proponents and opponents can come back together at some point and try again to resolve their differences.

Disagreeing without being disagreeable means remaining humble, respectful, and tactful in your interactions with people no matter what their point of view might be. You do not become angry or offensive when people disagree with you. However, it does not mean giving in to their arguments just to keep things from going awry. Linda Blaine had to learn this lesson before she could be an effective participant in arguments and debates.

Linda was an adept critical thinker. She was skilled at finding holes in arguments as well as recognizing bias, emotionalism, incomplete information, and inaccurate data. The problem was her approach to pointing these things out during an argument. Linda was prideful, egotistical, and came off as a know-it-all who thought everyone else was less capable than she was. She also became angry when people disagreed with her. This approach did not endear her to family members who suffered because of it.

Linda could turn a simple discussion about what to have for supper into a monumental feud. As a result, her husband and children avoided discussing anything with her. This isolated Linda in her own home. She had almost no verbal interaction with her family. One day she decided to talk to a friend about her problem. The friend told her, "Linda, you have got to learn to disagree without being disagreeable. Whether we are talking with teachers, the PTO, school board members, or fellow soccer moms, you lose it any time someone disagrees with you. You become angry, pushy, and offensive. This is why people will not talk with you about anything you might disagree with."

Linda thought about what her friend said about disagreeing without being disagreeable. Then she observed her friend discussing an issue about the curriculum at her children's school. Linda's friend disagreed with everything the other mother said, but she never lost her temper or became offensive. She was humble, respectful, and tactful. At the end of the conversation,

Linda's friend said, "Looks like we will have to agree to disagree."

Linda was fascinated by the exchange. She decided right then and there to try it. That night she asked her husband and children what they would like for supper. Their response was, "You decide. We don't want to argue about it." Linda told her family, "I understand, but that's not going to happen. There will be no argument, I guarantee it." Her family was surprised but decided to give the discussion a chance. They did not agree on what to have for supper, but Linda remained calm, humble, respectful, and tactful. She did not get angry, which surprised her children and shocked her husband. When it was obvious they were not going to agree, Linda said, "We will just have to agree to disagree. Why don't we just flip a coin." Things began to get better in Linda's household that very night.

SUMMARY

- The term *argument* suggests shouting matches in which people attack each other verbally and sometimes, physically. The resulting bitterness and resentment can ruin a relationship. This is why most people avoid arguments. But strife in not what arguments should be about. In the context of critical thinking, an argument is a discussion in which people try to better understand each other and their differing points of view. The maxim "steel sharpens steel" applies here. This is what happens in a productive argument. Arguing productively is an important critical thinking skill. Humility, respect, and tact are important in making arguments productive.
- Strategies for arguing productively include the following: do your research; never engage in a discussion without having fully researched the topic, do not argue about everything—some issues are not worth the effort; be humble, respectful, and tactful—your assertions and ideas will be

received more positively. Listen more and talk less—you will learn more by listening than talking; recognize verbal cunning—look for distortion, deceit, and lies in a proponent's argument; be brief and concise—brief feedback is received better than repetitive and verbose long-winded statements; compromise when it is acceptable—never compromise just to end an argument, but if there is common ground between the two sides, compromise may be a positive result of an argument; do not give up—work behind the scenes to resolve impasses in arguments. Disagree without being disagreeable—angry, pushy, egotistical know-it-alls contribute nothing to better decisions—sometimes you must agree to disagree.

16

RECOGNIZE AND REJECT LIES ON THE INTERNET

*I*f you use the internet or social media, you are being lied to. Count on it. Sorting out fact from fiction online and on social media may be the most difficult challenge critical thinkers face today. Without face-to-face discussions in which you can observe body language, nonverbal cues, emotionalism, biased language, and misdirection, it is much harder to know when someone is lying or distorting the message.

There are a lot of problems with the internet and social media including cyberbullying, information overload, social media addiction, fear of missing out, self-esteem issues, anxiety, and depression, but the most dangerous problem in the context of this book is purposeful deception, deceit, and lying. Other problems include a decrease in communication skills, subjection to fake news, sleeplessness, exposure to inappropriate content, and exposure to cyber-attacks. All these problems are worthy of discussion and analysis, but for the purpose of this book we will focus on disinformation, deception, distortion, and lies on the internet and social media.

DISINFORMATION ON THE INTERNET AND SOCIAL MEDIA

Disinformation is intentionally false input designed to influence readers to accept as fact a false point of view or assertion. Disinformation can be recognized when it cannot be validated, is written by non-experts, cannot be found on other internet or social media sites, and appeals to emotion rather than facts. The most common types of disinformation include propaganda, imposter content, biased information, misleading alerts or headlines, and information from government agencies. Examples of disinformation from government agencies pushing an agenda abound.

One can trust nothing that comes over the internet from China or Russia. Both restrict their citizens use of the internet and use it as a tool for limiting what can be learned about world events. In other words, they use it for state-sponsored propaganda. A good example of this is Russia's response to Vladimir Putin's brutal invasion of Ukraine. When Russian citizens protested the invasion, Putin cut off their internet access and filled the void with state-sponsored propaganda.

RECOGNIZING LIES AND DECEPTION ON THE INTERNET

The internet and social media are powerful enemies of truth. Since critical thinkers are dedicated to finding the truth and going wherever it leads, it is important to be able to recognize lies and deception on the internet and social media. What follows are some strategies you can use to separate fact from fiction when using the internet or social media.

NEVER BASE YOUR OPINION ON JUST ONE SOURCE

Be a personal fact-checker. Look at a variety of sources. Also consider the validity of the sources you check. Is the author of the information in question a recognized expert in his field? Check the author out. Does the information come from a reputable source you recognize? Can the information be validated by several different credible sources?

Kim Anderson is good at checking numerous sources before accepting what she reads online and on social media. First, she checks to see how many articles are available on the subject in question. Then she checks out the authors. After this, she looks inside the article to determine if the information is properly cited, lacking in emotion, and unbiased. As a result of her critical thinking and caution, Kim is rarely fooled by disinformation on the internet and social media.

DOES THE INFORMATION SEEM TOO GOOD OR TOO BAD TO BE TRUE?

Things that sound too good to be true usually are. The same rule of thumb applies to things that seem too bad to be true. The most common too-bad-to-be-true scenario is politicians attacking each other during political campaigns. Are there credible facts in the information, and are those facts backed by appropriate citations from credible sources? Never trust generalizations in information not supported by credible quotes, statistics, and other appropriately cited data.

Marco Castanza struggled with recognizing disinformation on the internet and social media. He was prone to believe things that sounded good about issues he agreed with and tended to disregard things that sounded bad about issues he agreed with. This caused Marco a major problem one day when he presented a proposal to his work team based on articles online. Once he stated his case, a critical thinker on his team tactfully pointed out the invalidity of his sources. It was an embarrassing moment for Marco; one that did not help his career.

AVOID EMOTIONAL THINKING

Even critical thinkers can fall prey to emotional thinking. You can see this in the news programs we watch. We tend to watch programs that reinforce our political and personal views. Assume you are a fan of a politician who is running for office. It will be easy to accept the positive stories about him on the internet or social media and disregard the negative stories. The problem with this is the positive stories may not be true while the negative stories might be. Rather than letting emotions influence your opinion, apply the same critical thinking strategies you apply to everything you read online and on social media.

Ramone Lopez listened to the same news program every night after work. He believed every word spoken on the program and would brook no challenges to his loyalty. He did not realize the program he favored had a political point of view and a political agenda. As a result, he took what was broadcast as the infallible truth—a mistake that came back to bite him. While sitting in the stands at his son's T-ball game, Ramone engaged several other parents in a discussion of the foibles of a politician he did not like. The information he held against the politician in question turned out to be false and his network news program had to apologize. Ramone did not see the broadcast in which the apology was made. When one of the other parents pointed it out to him, Ramone was embarrassed and a little angry at his own gullibility.

MAKE SURE YOU ARE NOT READING AN AD

Much of what you read online is sponsored material—ads camouflaged as valid content. Ads can be recognized by looking at the source line at the end of the article. Is the information provided by the company that manufactures the product in question or is it an independent source that is more likely to tell the truth? If you are unsure what you are reading is legitimate content, do a computer search in which you ask the following question: "Is product XYZ valid?" Several independent sites will pop up providing actual data about the product and the claims of its manufacturer.

Hanh Van Nguyen found out the hard way about sorting fact from fiction on the internet. He was looking for a good life insurance policy. The first one that popped up online sounded great, exceeding all expectations. Unfortunately, Hanh was reading—and falling for—a sponsored ad. Had he done a computer search in which he asked, "Is XYZ insurance policy legitimate?" he would have found out it was not. Instead, he found out the hard way by paying too much for a policy with limited coverage at best.

FACT-CHECK

Fact-checking is what critical thinkers do habitually. On the internet you can get help by going to fact-checking sites. These sites include PolitiFact which checks the accuracy of what politicians claim, Fact Check which also checks the accuracy of political claims, Snopes fact-checks news stories, and BBC Reality Check which also fact-checks news stories. Do not accept what any one of these sites claims without cross-checking with the other sites.

Donny Brunson learned to fact-check everything he read on the internet. Donny is a political junkie. He spends hours every day following news stories online. After being burned several times by false news stories, Donny started fact-checking everything he read, even information that sounded legitimate. This turned out to be a good approach. He even cross-checked the fact-checking sites he went to. Donny is seldom fooled by false information on the internet which has improved his reputation for accuracy in arguments and discussions.

ARTIFICIAL INTELLIGENCE—YOUR GREATEST CHALLENGE ON THE INTERNET

The greatest challenge critical thinkers face on the internet is artificial intelligence. Artificial intelligence (AI) is a new technology combining computer science and large databases to simulate human intelligence. An example of artificial intelligence becoming common is writing papers for college students and giving them answers to tests.

Artificial intelligence applications can turn out well-written papers on any subject in a matter of minutes or provide answers to test questions, and college professors have no answer for this kind of cheating. There are several problems with artificial intelligence, including its potential to eliminate jobs, possible use by terrorists, and intrusions on privacy. However, those explained herein are limited to problems that relate to the subject of this book: critical thinking.

- *Bias in artificial intelligence.* Artificial intelligence is created by human beings. This assures it will be biased. Human beings are prone to bias even when they try not to be. Bias can be conscious or unconscious. AI systems examine and use human decisions and human input to formulate their material. These decisions and input of humans are bound to be biased. In short, artificial intelligence is only as good as the input it takes in. The maxim "garbage in—garbage out" applies to artificial intelligence.
- *Intrusions on privacy.* Artificial intelligence watches people continually while tracking the data they reveal on the internet. By using our personal data, artificial intelligence systems can influence the decisions we make. For example, assume you ordered a product online. The next time you engage on social media, ads will pop up recommending other similar purchases. AI also invades smartphones, home speakers like Alexa, and any other technology that goes through the internet.
- *Difficulty in separating fact from fiction.* This is the downside of artificial intelligence—a troubling concern for critical thinkers. Someone preparing to make a presentation can download information created by artificial intelligence that looks viable, complete, and unbiased when it is none of

these things. Critical thinkers are devoted to digging out the truth, but AI makes it more difficult than any other factor to get at the truth.

RECOGNIZING LIES AND DISTORTIONS CREATED BY ARTIFICIAL INTELLIGENCE

Recognizing distortion, deception, and lies generated on the internet by artificial intelligence may be the most difficult task critical thinkers try to do. However, it can be done if you are willing to put in the time and effort. What you have to do is an intense version of fact-checking. To review, fact-checking means validating data and images to ensure they are complete, accurate, unbiased, and not slanted by emotionalism. It involves research, cross-referencing sources, assessing the validity of what you find in your research, and, sometimes, using fact-checking tools. The purpose of fact-checking is the same as the purpose of critical thinking: to ensure the best possible information to base decisions on. What follows are some strategies you can use to separate fact from fiction when dealing with information that might have been produced using artificial intelligence.

- *Look for irrelevant information.* Does the article you are reading contain irrelevant information? Does the information in the article seem flimsy or questionable? If so, discard the article and move on to others on the subject in question.
- *Make a list of questionable assertions.* As you go through articles on the internet, make a list of the questionable assertions and claims in them. Use this list as a reference as you seek out other articles on the same subject.
- *Look for suspicious numbers.* Does the article you are reading contain numbers that do not seem to add up? For example, does the article claim there are X number of Republicans in Florida when you know that number is wrong? Do other articles contain the same or a different number?

- *Look for suspicious dates.* Does the article you are reading contain dates that do not match dates you are familiar with. For example, if you are researching the life and death of Abraham Lincoln, are the dates of his birth and death accurate? How about other dates such as the date John Wilkes Booth shot him at Ford's Theatre? Is the date he signed the Emancipation Proclamation correct?
- *Review the entire document.* Once you apply the strategies recommended here, go over the entire document you are reading. Are there generalizations here where there should be hard facts? Is anything in the article at cross purposes with your intuition?
- *Check and double-check the sources cited.* To begin, are there any sources cited? With no sources cited, the article should be discarded. If there are sources, are they credible? The "Highly Cited" tool on Google will guide you to credible sources. Check to see if other articles on the same subject have used the same sources. If not, discard the article.

SUMMARY

- If you use the internet or social media, you are being lied to. Count on it. Sorting out fact from fiction online and on social media may be the most difficult challenge that critical thinkers face today. Without face-to-face discussions in which you can observe body language, nonverbal cues, emotionalism, biased language, and misdirection, it can be hard to know when someone is lying.
- The internet and social media contain much disinformation. Disinformation is intentionally false material intended to influence readers to accept as fact a false point of view or assertion. Disinformation can be recognized when it cannot be validated, is written by non-experts, cannot be found on other internet or social media sites, and appeals to emotion rather than facts.

- Recognizing lies, distortion, and deception online involves the following: 1) never basing your opinion on just one source; 2) asking if the information seems too good or too bad to be true; 3) avoiding emotional thinking; 4) making sure you are not reading an ad or other sponsored material; and 5) fact-checking.
- The biggest challenge critical thinkers face on the internet is artificial intelligence (AI). Artificial intelligence is a technology combining computer science and large databases to simulate human intelligence. An example of artificial intelligence becoming common is using AI to write papers for college students or to give them answers to test questions. Problems with artificial intelligence include bias, invasions of privacy, and difficulty in separating fact from fiction when the fiction was created using AI.
- Recognizing distortion, deception, and lies generated on the internet using artificial intelligence may be the most difficult challenge that critical thinkers face today. The following strategies will help critical thinkers identify and reject material produced using AI: 1) look for irrelevant information in anything you read on the internet; 2) make a list of questionable assertions you read; 3) look for suspicious numbers in the articles you read online; 4) look for suspicious dates; 5) once you have applied the other strategies explained herein, review the entire document you are reading to determine if there are generalizations where there should be hard facts and if the content is at cross purposes with your intuition; and 6) check and double-check all sources cited. The "Highly Cited" tool at Google will help with this last strategy.

17

DO NOT BE AFRAID TO THINK OBJECTIVELY

*T*here are numerous deterrents to critical thinking, most of which have been explained at length throughout this book. They include anxiety about rejection, uncertainty over how one's thoughts might be received, emotionalism, an aversion to details, a desire to fit into the group that is stronger than one's dedication to the truth, and several other factors. However, the most prominent deterrent to critical thinking might surprise you. It is fear. Some people fear thinking objectively. There are several reasons for this. The most important of these and how to overcome them are explained in this chapter.

WHY SOME PEOPLE FEAR THINKING OBJECTIVELY

There are four main factors that can cause people to fear thinking objectively. These factors are negative anticipation, anxiety over consequences, loss of control, and public speaking. Several additional deterrents turn people away from critical thinking. Let us look at each of these factors individually.

NEGATIVE ANTICIPATION

With this fear-causing factor, people anticipate bad things happening if they think objectively. Those bad things might be rejection, hurt feelings, or exclusion from the group. Consider the following example of an individual who refuses to engage in critical thinking because she fears what might happen if she does.

Isabel Garcia has all the skills to be a talented critical thinker. She is a good researcher, has common sense, and can recognize bias, emotionalism, and distortion. However, she refuses to apply her critical thinking skills out of fear of what might happen if she does. When her team at work discusses new proposals and recommendations for improvement, Isabel sits quietly without offering any input or feedback. She takes the proceedings in and knows if the presenter is sincere or just pushing a personal agenda. Isabel knows when she is being lied to. Unfortunately for her work team, she fears hurting the feelings of those she might challenge and, in turn, being rejected by them. This hurts her team and her employer because her input could lead to better decisions.

FEAR OF CONSEQUENCES

With this factor, people fear their input and feedback might lead to bad decisions that could come back to haunt them. It is not that they cannot think objectively, they fear offering feedback which might cause problems that undermine quality, productivity, efficiency, and effectiveness or put them in a position of appearing foolish. They simply have no confidence in themselves. Consider the following example of an individual who refuses to apply critical thinking skills out of fear of imagined consequences.

Kai Lin has the skills necessary to be a good critical thinker. Unfortunately, he lacks the confidence to apply those skills. During meetings with his fellow soccer coaches, Kai will sometimes quietly comment to another coach, but he steadfastly refuses to stand up and provide feedback or input into discussions. This is too bad for his soccer team because Kai knows the game better than any of the other coaches. Despite his advanced knowledge of soccer, Kai is afraid a suggestion he makes might cause his team to lose a game. As a result, his team loses out on a tremendous asset that could help them win more games.

LOSS OF CONTROL

People want to have control over the situations they find themselves in. They want to think they can prevent negative consequences, hurt feelings, rejection, and exclusion from the group. But the truth is we rarely have complete control over the events in our lives. For this reason, some people who could be excellent critical thinkers hold back because they fear a loss of control. They fear they will not be able to avoid negative consequences. Consider the following example of an individual who refuses to think objectively out of fear of losing control and incurring negative consequences.

Matias Arballo was quick to see through false arguments and to recognize distortion, deception, and lies. Unfortunately, Matias was not one to speak up and point out discrepancies in the arguments of others. Matias liked to be in control of the situations he participated in. If he knew or even sensed he would not be, Matias would hold back and not participate in discussions or debates. As a result, his work team missed out on what could have been valuable, relevant input and feedback from Matias.

PUBLIC SPEAKING

Believe it or not, public speaking is the number one fear of American adults. Some people—a lot of them—fear public speaking more than taxes, snakes, spiders, and even death. People who fear public speaking would rather do almost anything than stand up in public and state their views before an audience large or small. Consider the following example of an individual who has excellent critical thinking skills but will not put them to use out of fear of public speaking.

Bart Sumlin was particularly adept at seeing through the fog of distortion, deception, and lies that sometimes occurred in his book club. People who had not even read the assigned book would make grand pronouncements about its content, meaning, and symbology. Bart knew when he was being fed a line by an insincere member of the group and often disagreed with the presenter, but he let it all roll off him like water off a duck. There was no way he was going to stand up in front of a group and make his views known.

In addition, Bart never participated as a presenter no matter how much his fellow book club members encouraged him to. When he attempted public speaking in the past, the same thing always happened. His hands began to sweat, his mouth got dry, his whole body shook, and he could not remember his own name much less any information he hoped to convey. Bart's aversion to public speaking robbed his book club of the insights of a bright man who could explain the author's intentions better than anyone else in the group.

OVERCOMING FEAR OF THINKING OBJECTIVELY

If you fear thinking objectively, do not fret about it. You can overcome the factors holding you back. What follows in this section are strategies for overcoming the fear of thinking objectively. If you apply these strategies consistently and regularly, you will overcome any fear you may have of joining in discussions and debates as a critical thinker who contributes to better decisions.

OVERCOMING NEGATIVE ANTICIPATION AND FEAR OF CONSEQUENCES

These two fears are closely related. Both turn people away from critical thinking for fear of uncomfortable consequences. The consequences might be rejection, exclusion from the group, criticism, being laughed at, or providing input that might lead to failure. To overcome these two fears, it is necessary to ask, "What is the worst that can happen?" and understand most of the things we worry about never happen.

A lot of people waste a lot of time worrying about things that never happen or, when they do, are not nearly as negative as anticipated. If you are humble, tactful, and respectful, the negative consequences you fear will not come to pass most of the time, but if they do, the consequences are likely to be less than you anticipated. However, if you are ever subjected to such consequences as ad hominem attacks or exclusion, remember this: you do not need the approval or inclusion of people who resort to these things.

Sofia Calderon never participated in discussions or debates in her college classes out of fear of negative consequences. Sofia is conservative while most of her classmates are liberal, at least the most vocal of them. She is constantly taken aback by some of the views of her liberal classmates. She wants to speak out, but just cannot make herself do it; not, that is, until a classmate began to argue that the basic education classes they were required to take—English, mathematics, history, and science—were a waste of time. Without realizing she was doing it, Sofia stood up and defended the basics claiming students were not learning to read or write in high school so it was even more important than it had ever been that they learn the basics in college. "If this institution starts graduating students who cannot read their own diplomas, it will hurt all of us."

To her surprise, several other people in class joined the discussion on her side. After several more joined Sofia, the student who thought the basics were a waste of time relented and claimed he needed to think the issue through further. Sofia's fears never manifested themselves, and she soon became an adept critical thinker.

OVERCOMING THE FEAR OF A LOSS OF CONTROL

People like to be in control of their circumstances, although they seldom are. One of the reasons some people fear being critical thinkers is they are afraid a discussion or debate might get out of hand; they might lose control. Lonnie MacIntosh liked to be in control. He grew up in a single-parent home with a mother who worked two jobs and drank to excess. From a young age, Lonnie had to take control of the household and his two younger brothers. If he did not, there would be no meals, homework would go undone, and the house would be a mess.

When he went to work, Lonnie brought his need to be in control with him. This is why he feared being a critical thinker. He observed discussions and debates devolve into arguments in which participants lost control of their emotions and verbally attacked each other. He wanted none of that. He discussed this dilemma with a fellow employee whose opinions he respected. His friend told him, "Lonnie, what is the worst that can happen? If things get out of control, you can just step back and let the others attack each other. You don't have to join in."

Acting on this advice, Lonnie began to join in discussions and debates at work. To his surprise, things seldom got out of control; and the few times they did, he took his friend's advice and stepped back. He let others in the room attack each other. By remaining calm and refusing to get into verbal scrapes with colleagues, Lonnie became a well-respected member of the team whose critical thinking was appreciated by his colleagues.

OVERCOMING THE FEAR OF PUBLIC SPEAKING

Of the various fears of being a critical thinker, fear of public speaking may be the most difficult to overcome. Speaking up in meetings carries the same level of fear for many people. To speak up in meetings over issues and proposals, you must speak publicly. This does not mean you have to give speeches to large audiences, although some people find the intimacy and closeness of small group meetings even more forbidding. If you are one of the many people who fears speaking publicly, do not be discouraged. You can overcome this fear; many have. What follows in this section are several strategies you can use to overcome the fear of public speaking. Doing so usually takes time, so give it the time needed. Do not rush, and do not jump in all at once.

- *Do your research.* The better you know the topic in question, the more confident you will be speaking up about it. Do your research, know your topic, and make good notes to which you can easily refer when speaking.
- *Practice what you might need to say.* Assume you are in a group setting and the group is discussing a proposal. Practice speaking up as if others are not in the room. Tactfully challenge an assertion you think the presenter might make. Do this over and over until you become comfortable with it.
- *Put aside specific worries.* Make a list of what worries you most about public speaking. Then ask yourself, "What is the worst that could happen?" about each item on the list. Remember most of the things we worry about never happen in the first place. Those that do are seldom as bad as we anticipated.
- *Take a few deep breaths before speaking.* Once you decide to give speaking in public a chance, take a few deep breaths before starting. This will help settle your nerves.
- *Get comfortable with silence.* Once you speak up in a public meeting, the response may be silence. Do not worry about silence. There are a lot of reasons why silence is sometimes the reaction you get after commenting on a presenter's proposal. One of the reasons is the presenter simply does not know how to respond.

Juan Garcia feared public speaking more than anything he could name. Just the thought of it made his hands sweat and his heart beat faster. Yet, he longed to engage in discussions of how to improve the performance of the high school volleyball team he served as an assistant coach. Knowing Juan's prowess when it came to volleyball strategy and his ability to motivate players, one of his fellow coaches told Juan, "You need to speak up. We need your input."

Just hearing this made Juan nervous. But Juan decided right then and there to do what was necessary to overcome his fear of speaking in public. He knew his material well already. Consequently, he began participating in make-believe discussions and debates in his office. He did this every day for weeks. Finally, Juan was ready to join his fellow coaches in discussions of strategy. When he did, Juan was nervous but took a few deep breaths and jumped in. When the discussion of strategies was over, the head coach pulled Juan aside and said, "It's about time you joined these discussions. We need your input."

REDUCING THE NEGATIVE CONSEQUENCES OF CRITICAL THINKING

In addition to the strategies presented so far for overcoming the fear of public speaking, there are several other strategies you can use to reduce the negative consequences of speaking in public meetings. These strategies are explained in this section.

PRACTICE, PRACTICE, AND PRACTICE

When you are present in discussions of issues, assertions, points of view, and proposals, silently practice the critical thinking skills taught in this book. You do not need to speak up just yet. Build your confidence by silently noting when you recognize the information being presented is biased, incomplete, inaccurate, or based on emotion. Over time you will gain the confidence you need to speak up. When you do, be tactful and respectful of the presenter whose arguments you may have to refute. Practice will eliminate the fear of looking foolish and making invalid challenges or recommendations.

Consider the following example of a critical thinker who failed to use her skills to help the local school board make better decisions.

Melissa Gilroy took her responsibility of motherhood seriously. She wanted to be with her kids rather than work an outside job, so the family of six was on a tight budget. That meant paying for private school wasn't possible and the expense involved with homeschooling was just more than they could handle. Melissa knew about some of the pitfalls of the public school system, but the schools in their quasi-rural area were pretty good. Nonetheless, Melissa attended every PTO meeting and started attending school board meetings. She never sought leadership positions because of her shyness so her perspective was from the outside. At a recent board meeting, the topic of discussion was Critical Race Theory. The presenter assured those in attendance this was a great curriculum designed to teach the children how bad racism is. Several things he said seemed odd and a little off to Melissa but she remained quiet and asked no questions, only after the curriculum was implemented did Melissa discover the true nature of CRT. She stood up to the principal of her oldest son's high school and pressed the issue with the PTO and the school board and many parents followed her lead. With every confrontation, Melissa was better informed and she delivered her arguments with respect. Critical thinking became Melissa's strong suit as a mom and citizen.

PRACTICE HUMILITY, RESPECT, AND TACT

One of the reasons discussions and debates sometimes go awry and turn into shouting matches is how opponents of the presenter's proposal state their challenges. If the feedback you give sounds more like criticism than helpful feedback, some proponents are going to become defensive and resentful. This is when things can devolve into a bad scene, which is one of the reasons some people are reluctant to take part in discussions. Do not let this be a problem for you. You can reduce the possibility of shouting matches, anger, frustration, and resentment by how you state your challenges.

The key to becoming good at speaking out during meetings without causing hard feelings is to be humble, respectful, and tactful. Nothing you can do will go further than this in making sure your feedback is given due consideration without frustration or resentment. Humility means a lack of pride or arrogance. Modesty is a synonym for humility. Respect means regard for the feelings, wishes, and rights of others. Consideration and thoughtfulness are synonyms for respect. Tact means sensitivity in working with others on difficult issues. Synonyms are delicacy and thoughtfulness.

Ming-Na conquered her fear of speaking in public meetings by practicing not just what she might say, but how she might say it. She wanted to make sure her feedback was offered in the best possible way. When she finally decided to offer feedback in a meeting, Ming-Na saw there were holes in the presenter's proposal big enough to drive a truck through. But instead of saying that, she began with, "I can see you have put a lot of work into your proposal and you make several excellent points. If I may, I would like to offer a few suggestions that might make your proposal even stronger. I will be happy to meet with you after the meeting to discuss feedback if that would be more comfortable for you."

Ming-Na's humility, respect, and tact became legend in her company. As a result, presenters welcomed her feedback and even sought her out before making presentations. Even presenters with a reputation for blowing up and attacking challengers stayed on an even keel when Ming-Na offered suggestions. They appreciated her humility and respect, which made them open to listening to her and giving due consideration to her tactful challenges.

SUMMARY

- There are numerous deterrents to critical thinking. They include anxiety about rejection, uncertainty over how one's thoughts will be received, emotionalism, aversion to details, a desire to fit into a group being stronger than one's commitment to the truth, fear of public speaking, and several other factors. However, the most prominent deterrent to critical thinking is fear. Some people fear thinking objectively.

- There are four main factors that can cause people to fear thinking objectively: 1) negative anticipation occurs when people anticipate bad things happening; 2) fear of consequences occurs when people fear their input and feedback might lead to bad decisions that could come back to haunt them; 3) loss of control occurs when a meeting goes awry and the presenter loses control.

- Overcoming the fear of public speaking involves doing your research on the topic in question, practicing what you might say, putting aside specific worries, taking a few deep breaths before speaking, and getting comfortable with silence. Reducing the potential negative consequences of objective speaking involve practicing what you plan to say with humility, respect, and tact.

18

IS THE BIBLE A RELIABLE SOURCE OF TRUTH?

*T*his may be the most difficult chapter in this book. Christians have learned when Jesus Christ walked the earth in human form, He walked truth into the world, but God was truth even before He sent His only Son to show us the way. In Luke 16:17, the apostle writes it is easier for heaven and earth to pass away than for any word from the Bible to be untrue. Eventually, Jesus left us with the Holy Bible as our source of truth. He speaks truth to us through Scripture. This does not mean there are no truths outside the Bible. Gravity, for instance, is not specifically dealt with in Scripture, but it is true and it is a fact. But what makes gravity and other facts that come from outside the Bible true is they align with biblical truths.

Unbelievers who read this book may find it difficult to accept the Bible as the only real, immutable, and permanent source of truth. We understand this but be careful. There are plenty of people who think they are intellectually superior, and who believe the Bible is a book of myths. These people find the truth of the Bible offensive because it challenges their egotistical opinion of themselves. Do not be one of these. Those who place themselves above God stride to their doom.

You can believe the Bible because it was written by Jesus Christ, not human beings with agendas, false motives, and biased opinions. Human beings transcribed the Bible, but Jesus dictated it; He breathed it out. Psalm 12:6 says the words of the Lord are pure and compares them to silver that has been refined in a furnace and purified seven times. This is why believers can follow the admonition in 2 Corinthians to destroy lofty opinions that run counter to the Word of God. This is done by thinking objectively and relying on the Bible as your source of truth.

If you struggle with the Bible being the permanent, unchanging source of truth, keep an open mind, read this chapter objectively, and give the message an opportunity to sink in. You are going to find as you become a skilled critical thinker that having an unchanging source of truth will help you overcome the "not your truth but my truth" syndrome where individuals decide for themselves what is true and what is false. Even to the most ardent unbeliever, this syndrome represents an idea that cannot be justified. If every individual on earth can decide what is true or false, there can be 7.88 billion (and counting) versions of the truth. This is why we need one real and immutable source of truth, and the Bible is that source.

There are biblical truths pertaining to every critical thinking skill presented in this book. In this chapter we explain the biblical foundation of critical thinking. The veracity, honesty, and accuracy of what the Bible has to say about critical thinking form the basis for this concept as a process for persistently pursuing the truth in all situations.

BIBLICAL TRUTHS ABOUT CRITICAL THINKING

Critical thinking allows people to measure the validity of claims, assertions, ideas, and proposals against the truths found in the Bible; truths that stand up to even the most detailed examinations. This is why Christians who are critical thinkers are not afraid to be asked hard questions because the Bible gives them solid, irrefutable answers.

Critical thinkers must be more than knowledgeable, they must also be wise. Proverbs 1:7 tells us fear of the Lord is the beginning of wisdom. In biblical terms, "fear of the Lord" does not mean being afraid of Him, but rather it means submitting to Him in humility, faith, and respect. There were false prophets in biblical times and there are false prophets now. These are people who will deceive, distort, and lie to get their way. The Bible is clear on how we are to deal with false prophets. In 1 John 4:1, we are told to avoid believing every spirit, but rather to test the spirits to see whether they are from God or from false prophets. This verse could be the motto of critical thinkers.

Jesus established the biblical basis for critical thinking when He gave us Isaiah 1:18 where He says, come and let us reason together. Critical thinking is all about reason, logic, and common sense. Proverbs 14:15 states the naïve believe anything they hear, but the prudent are more careful. The prudent in this case are critical thinkers. The fact that Jesus would admonish us to reason together means honest reasoning, logic, and common sense should be the basis for arguments, discussions, and debates. There is no room for deception, distortion, and lying in Jesus's approach to arguing.

BIBLICAL TRUTHS ABOUT BIAS

The Bible often uses the term *partiality* to indicate bias. When people are partial, they are biased toward one party or point of view and toward one side of the question in arguments. They favor something without reason. The Bible is clear in denouncing bias. James 2:1 admonishes us to practice our faith without showing partiality. The Bible also uses the terms *favoritism*, *snobbery*, and *elitism* as synonymous with bias

You may not think of snobbery as bias, but it is. The bias comes from the egos of the person or group that engages in snobbery. Snobbery says, "We are better than you." For example, it is not uncommon for highly educated people such as college professors to look down on people who do not share their level of educational achievement. What they do not acknowledge is education and wisdom are not the same thing. There are a lot of highly educated fools in the world, many of them college professors who think they are intellectually superior to God. God is concerned about our level of wisdom, not our level of education.

Another example of snobbery can be found in the church. There are fellow Christians who are always pointing out the shortcomings of others while acting holier than thou. This kind of religious snobbery shuts down fellowship and turns people away from the church. Religious snobs think they are righteous when, in fact, they are self-righteous. They need to study the Bible they use as a weapon instead of a tool. This kind of behavior on the part of church members is why it is sometimes said. "It's a wonder Christianity has survived Christians."

Here is an example of snobbery that eventually, but painfully, led to a happy ending. Professor Gilmore felt when he was awarded his PhD he been anointed. He was at the pinnacle of his academic discipline, a truly superior human being. Overnight, Gilmore turned into an academic snob. His snobbery was so noticeable even colleagues, some of them academic snobs, were turned off by Gilmore's superior attitude.

The janitor for Gilmore's building, Washington Reid, was a devoted Christian and a deacon in his church. Gilmore would occasionally see Washington kneeling in prayer. Further, Washington often greeted Gilmore with, "Good morning, sir. God bless you." Professor Gilmore, who was a not a happy man, thought Washington appeared to be the happiest person on campus—something he could not understand. Washington had no education and lived close to the poverty line, yet he was the most helpful person Gilmore ever saw. He was always doing something to help professors and students. Gilmore, on the other hand, did not get along with his colleagues and hated students, especially those who disagreed with him or did not accept his condescending attitude.

People liked Washington and gravitated to him. He was a good listener, so they often shared their troubles, hopes, and dreams with him. Washington gave everyone he talked to good biblical advice and encouragement. Professor Gilmore, on the other hand, was avoided by colleagues and students who did not enjoy being talked down to and treated like inferior beings.

Professor Gilmore often criticized Washington for praying to "a God that does not exist," calling the Bible a "fictional book of myths." Washington always responded to these attacks in the same way. He smiled at the professor and said, "I pray every day God will show you the light so you can see the world more clearly. You have a lot of knowledge, but God will give you wisdom."

Professor Gilmore continued his egotistical snobbery and Washington kept praying for him. Then, one day, tragedy struck. Gilmore's wife and only son were killed in an automobile accident by a drunk driver who was driving the wrong way down a one-way street. Gilmore was overcome with grief and sunk into a deep state of depression. He could barely function and was forced to take a leave of absence from the university.

Observing the professor's grief, Washington, who lost his wife two years earlier, mobilized his church. Its members brought meals to Gilmore's home, prayed for him, ran errands, cleaned his house, and did his yard work. Gilmore, who had a rough upbringing, had never been treated with such kindness, caring, and love. Before long, he began to open to Washington and talk with him for hours. Gilmore told Washington he thought God was punishing him for turning his back on the church and being such a snob. The janitor explained the love of God to Gilmore and how in a fallen world bad things can happen, an often do, to good people.

God did not dictate his wife and son's death, but He would make sure something good came out of it. Relieved of guilt, Gilmore asked if he could join Washington at church that Sunday. He did, and before long he surrendered to Christ, was baptized, and joined the church. Two years later, after pursuing biblical truth with more fervor than any academic study, Gilmore was a deacon, and a much humbler man. He and Washington became as close as two people can be. Gilmore's colleagues often saw the professor and janitor praying together before sharing lunch.

BIBLICAL TRUTHS ABOUT HUMAN MOTIVES

A motive is a reason for acting, making a choice, or adopting an opinion. Human motives tend to be self-serving. We are all driven by human motives. You will recall Maslow's Hierarchy of Needs in which the psychologist identified five basic needs all humans have: physiological, safety, love, belonging, esteem, and self-actualization. The Bible has much to say about human motives. Motives can be good or bad. Those aligning with Scripture are good motives, and those that do not are bad motives.

Proverbs 21:2 warns that every man is right in his own estimation (because he sees through self-serving eyes), but God weighs the heart. In other words, God knows our motives no matter what we do to disguise them. In 1 Corinthians 15:58, we are admonished to avoid being moved by self-serving human motives, but to give our work to the Lord. We are to be motivated by a desire to serve the Lord. In James 4:3 we are told when we ask of God, we will not receive if we ask with wrong motives such as spending our requests on hedonistic pleasures.

When people try to push an agenda, receive approval of a proposal, or validate assertions based on a self-serving agenda, they violate the biblical teachings of Christ. They distort the truth to get what they want when what God wants is for us to serve Him and His children. Critical thinkers, on the other hand, follow the truth wherever it leads.

BIBLICAL TRUTHS ABOUT EXPLANATIONS VERSUS RATIONALIZATIONS

Rationalization is a defense mechanism in which people substitute false statements to conceal the truth. For example, an individual who is turned down for membership in a college fraternity might claim defensively, "I did not want to get into that crummy fraternity anyway." In truth, this individual is deeply disappointed. He badly wanted to be a member of the fraternity.

Proverbs 12:22 makes clear that lying lips are an abomination to the Lord. Rationalizing is just another form of lying. Ephesians 4:25 admonishes us to put away falsehoods and speak the truth. Proverbs 28:13 tells us those who conceal their transgressions will fail, but those who confess their transgressions will receive mercy. Our transgressions—which include rationalizing—are the sinful behavior some engage in, such as lust, lying, anger, impatience, ego, and self-centeredness. These are just some of the kinds of transgressions people try to rationalize.

Hong Tran is a master rationalizer. He can justify almost anything he has done wrong by rationalizing it. Resorting to rationalizing every time one of his transgressions came to the surface, got Hong by in the past, but recently his rationalizing caught up with him. When it was pointed out that a proposal he submitted at work contained major holes in it—holes he should have known about and, in reality did—Hong claimed, "I could have done more research if our boss didn't ride me so hard every day." This rationalization did not sit well with his colleagues, but it was soon overshadowed by an even worse problem. Hong was caught stealing from his employer. He tried to rationalize his illegal behavior by claiming, "If this company paid me what I'm worth I would not have to steal." Hong was fired that day.

BIBLICAL TRUTHS ABOUT RESEARCH

Critical thinkers do research to ferret out the truth in arguments, proposals, opinions, points of view, and assertions. This is what research is for right-minded people: a search for the truth. The truth cannot be elusive and hard to find. This is why the more you read the Bible the better you will be at using it to identify the truth in any given situation.

Researching a subject before discussing or debating it is essential because there are so many people who try to distort the truth when arguing a given point of view pushing a hidden agenda. In John 8:32, Jesus said if you obey his Word, you will know the truth and the truth will set you free. In order to obey God's Word, you must study it and know what it says. The Bible is even more than the trove of wisdom and knowledge; it tells us who God is and His plan for all creation, including man.

Research can be the best friend of critical thinkers because people generally find it difficult to admit they are wrong. The truth can hurt. When it does, people go into defensive mode to protect themselves and their opinions. Research can give you the hard facts to show truth to people who struggle with admitting they are wrong. They need to learn to heed the words of Jesus in John 14:6 where He declares He is the way, the truth, and the life. No one can come to the Father except though Him.

BIBLICAL TRUTHS ABOUT SHORT-TERM EXPEDIENTS

Short-term expedients are not necessarily bad things, provided they are followed up with permanent solutions. It's only when they are put in place and forgotten about or when they are chosen over long-term solutions out of laziness that they become problematic. The Bible has much to say about adopting short-term expedients. For example, Proverbs 31:14 states that the wise woman brings her food from far away. In other words, she plans ahead thinking of the long-term rather than the short-term. In this way, she does not have to rely on last-minute decisions that lead to short-term expedients.

Proverbs 21:5 states the diligent plan ahead, but the hasty fall short. The "hasty" in this verse are those who propose short-term expedients over long-term solutions. Perhaps the best-known verses in the Bible about being wise instead of expedient is the story of the ant in Proverbs 6:6–11. In these verses we are told to consider the example of the ant. It prepares food in the summer and gathers its harvest. In other words, the ant looks ahead and plans for permanent solutions rather than short-term expedients.

BIBLICAL TRUTHS ABOUT SEPARATING FACTS FROM OPINIONS

Separating facts from opinions is an important skill for critical thinkers because much of what you hear in arguments, discussions, and debates is opinion, not fact. Conclusions based on opinions will inevitably fail. Proverbs 18:2 is clear on the issue. It states a fool does not seek understanding, but instead seeks to express his opinion. In 1 Kings 18:21, Elijah minced no words when it comes to facts versus opinions. In effect, he asked the people, "How long will you equivocate bouncing, back and forth between different opinions? If the Lord is God, follow Him. If Baal is God, follow him." This is important because biblical truth is bigger than just facts. A biblical truth is a fact augmented by belief in the One who is the truth.

BIBLICAL TRUTHS ABOUT COMMON SENSE

What we call common sense, the Bible calls wisdom. Wisdom is more than knowledge, although knowledge is a component of wisdom. The other components are insight, good judgment, experience, and generally accepted beliefs. The generally accepted beliefs must be those that align with the Bible. They cannot be beliefs generally held by unbelievers and those who reject the truth of Scripture. Proverbs 16:22 states good sense is the fountain of life, but the instruction of those who reject Scripture is folly.

Unlike his fellow city council members, Derrick Strand had no education beyond high school. What he did have was common sense and lots of it. His insights were usually spot-on and his judgment good. In addition, he had years of experience and his beliefs came from Scripture. Because of this, his participation in discussions and arguments among city council members was invaluable. His participation usually kept the city council on an even keel. That is what he was trying to do at the most recent meeting of the council.

Despite the problems other big cities were having with a spike in crime after defunding their police departments, the chairman of the city council wanted to cut back on his city's police force and use the money saved to hire social workers and counselors. Common sense argued against such a proposal. The last meeting turned into a debate between the council chair and Derrick. The council chair argued that hiring social workers and counselors would help get at the root of the problem, and police officers were qualified to do nothing more than lock criminals up.

Derrick countered that criminals should be locked up. Then he asked the council chair a series of common-sense questions. How will counselors and social workers prevent mobs from looting stores? How will counselors prevent thugs from attacking and robbing old ladies on the street? How will counselors prevent little children from being caught in the crossfire of rival gangs? What do you think will happen to your counselors and social workers if they venture into the wrong side of town to do their work?

Derrick concluded his statements by saying, "Mr. Chairman, the first step is to stop the crimes. For that we need police officers and plenty of them patrolling the streets. The second step is counseling and social work. If you mix the two steps up or leave the first one out, you are going to have dead counselors and social workers on your hands." The city council voted to retain and expand its police department.

BIBLICAL TRUTHS ABOUT AD HOMINEM ARGUMENTS

The Bible warns against interacting with people who engage in ad hominem attacks. Ad hominem arguments are directed at a person's character to invalidate his arguments. They claim, in so many words, there is something objectionable about anyone who disagrees with them. For example, consider this ad hominem attack on Gomez Garcia. "You cannot believe anything Gomez says. What does he know? He never even finished high school."

The Bible rejects ad hominem arguments, as do critical thinkers. For example, 2 Timothy 2:23 admonishes us to avoid stupid and foolish arguments because they just become quarrels. How do you avoid ad hominem arguments? First, be respectful, humble, and tactful in your disagreement. Second, ignore the attack as one coming from a child. Second Timothy 2:16–17 states those who engage in irreverent speech produce only godlessness. The ad hominem attacker will sooner or later pay a price for his foolishness.

BIBLICAL TRUTHS ABOUT THE CANCEL CULTURE

Recall the cancel culture involves rejecting or failing to support someone because they have a different point of view offensive to some—although the supposed offensive is often manufactured. In practical terms, it means being censored on social media, boycotted as a business, or attacked as an individual lacking in character. The cancel culture is not new to Christians. The Bible is replete with examples of believers who were killed, exiled, or ridiculed for speaking out against authorities.

The prophets of the Lord were often targets of authorities who rejected Jesus. In 1 Kings 18:4 we learn Queen Jezebel killed the prophets of the Lord for speaking what was offensive to her. In Jeremiah 20:1–2, the prophet was captured, beaten, shackled, and thrown into a cistern of mud to die for saying what was unpopular with authorities. In 1 Kings 22:1–40 the prophet Micaiah was beaten and imprisoned for telling King Ahab a truth he did not want to hear. God's response to the cancel culture is we should be swift to hear and slow to speak. We should also resist becoming angry and wrathful against those who censor or cancel us (James 1:19–20). We are to avoid becoming like them.

BIBLICAL TRUTHS ABOUT OVERSIMPLIFICATION

The Bible warns against oversimplification of arguments because that is precisely what a lot of people do when reading Scripture, making proposals, arguing opinions, or pushing an agenda. They take Bible verses out of context and interpret them in self-serving ways. In doing so, Christians often set one passage of Scripture against other passages. This is a mistake. The Bible never contradicts itself. Oversimplification leads to inaccurate and false interpretations of the Bible and on the part of people making a proposal or pushing an agenda.

Consider the following examples of oversimplification in the Bible. Philippians 4:13 tells us we can do anything through Christ. This verse is often oversimplified to mean I can become anything and do anything if I am faithful to Christ. The problem with this oversimplification is that it leads believers astray. A person who is puny and lacking in talent is not going to become an NFL star no matter how closely he follows Jesus. We cannot do any worldly thing or everything we want through Christ. What the verse really means is God will give us the strength and guidance needed to follow His will. Remember, many things are allowed but not all things are helpful. A person's desire to do or become anything she wants may be allowable but not helpful.

Another verse often misinterpreted because of over simplification is Matthew 7:1 where the Bible tells us not to judge others or we will be judged. This verse, taken in context, warns against judging people for the same sins you commit. It is a guard against hypocrisy and self-righteousness. It is not a warning against being discerning about the behavior and views of other people. In fact, the Bible tells us to rebuke sinners and teach them a better way.

Pierre Fanchant was the king of oversimplification. At first it worked well for him when arguing politics with friends and colleagues. However, after a while it became obvious oversimplification was a strategy used to deceive and distort. When the issue of transgendered males competing against women in athletic events came up, Pierre claimed, "It's simply a matter of choosing who you want to be. If you choose to be a woman, you should be able to compete against women." Of course, his oversimplified argument left out a lot of important facts. Because of his propensity for oversimplifying complicated and nuanced arguments, people eventually dismissed Pierre's arguments as meaningless.

BIBLICAL TRUTHS ABOUT INCONVENIENT TRUTHS AND UNCOMFORTABLE FACTS

The Bible has much to say about avoiding uncomfortable truths and inconvenient facts because a lot of what is said in Scripture makes sinners—meaning all of us—uncomfortable. Avoiding inconvenient truths and uncomfortable facts comes naturally to people. We do not like to hear bad news. This is why some people refrain from going to a doctor even though they feel bad. They are afraid of what the problem might be, and do not want to hear it. It is why some presenters will leave relevant information out of their proposals. The relevant information in question reveals inconvenient truths and uncomfortable facts they do not want you to hear.

One of the most inconvenient truths in the Bible is if you reject Jesus, you are going to hell, which is to be eternally separated from God and every good thing He created. People do not want to hear this truth, so they turn away from Christianity and the Bible (2 Peter 3:7). In Matthew 13:47–50, we read that at the close of the age angels will separate evil people from the righteous. Evil people will be thrown into a fiery furnace. In 2 Peter 3:5 we read that some people prefer to remain willingly ignorant of this biblical truth. In the days of Noah, his neighbors did not want to hear the inconvenient truth and uncomfortable fact that God was going to flood the entire earth. Refusing to hear inconvenient truths and uncomfortable facts cost them their lives.

BIBLICAL TRUTHS ABOUT DISTORTED CONCLUSIONS

The Bible has much to say about distorted conclusions because the Bible is often distorted to make it more palatable to sinners who do not want to obey God's Word. Sad to say, some of the most egregious distorters of biblical truth are pastors who are trying to conform their churches to the world rather than having the world conform to God's Word. In 2 Peter 3:16 we read how ignorant and unstable people purposely distort and their distortions will eventually lead to their destruction.

People arrive at distorted conclusions when they twist, ignore, water down, restate truth to be less offensive to people who reject the truth or try to be politically correct based on the anti-Christian sensibilities of contemporary culture. Distortion is the opposite of seeking the truth. In 2 Timothy 3:16 we read that all Scripture comes from God. This means anything that challenges, rejects, or distorts Scripture is wrong. The Bible is our source of truth. It is accurate and immutable. People who use verbal ruses to distort conclusions in business meetings, education, government, or any other field of endeavor are subverting the truth.

BIBLICAL TRUTHS ABOUT ARGUING PRODUCTIVELY

Productive arguments are those in which both sides come to a better understanding of the issue and, as a result, can make better suggestions for a positive conclusion. But pride often gets in the way of productive arguments. When humility, respect, and tact are replaced by arrogance and pride, the argument is not likely to be productive. Arrogance and pride breed contempt for the other person's views and, sometimes, for the other person.

The Bible has much to say about arguing productively. In Proverbs 15:1 we read how a soft answer turns away contempt, but harsh words stir up anger. Philippians 2:14 warns us to avoid griping and disputing. Romans 14:19 is the quintessential verse on arguing productively. It states we should pursue peace, mutual understanding, and building each other up.

Denver Andrews, a critical thinker, was a master at arguing productively. As a college dean, he was an old-fashioned liberal; meaning, he welcomed different points of view and enjoyed interacting with people who disagreed with each other on the larger issues of the day. Denver, a Christian, had a plaque on the wall of his office quoting Proverbs 3:30 warning us to avoid contending with others for no reason and when they have done no harm. Denver lived by Proverbs 3:30 when it came to arguing.

His approach to argumentation came in handy when the Republican club invited a conservative politician to speak on campus. Leftwing students were apoplectic in their opposition. They loudly promised protests. Some of the more radical among them even threatened to do harm to the speaker. Leftwing student leaders were big fans of Denver. As a man who debated some of the biggest named conservatives—including people who later became presidential candidates—Denver was their guru. These Leftist student leaders stormed into Denver's office demanding he cancel the event. Denver invited them to sit down. Then, he listened to their views on allowing a conservative to speak on campus.

When they finished, Denver told them two things. First, he told them if they rioted and canceled the event, they were not real liberals. Real liberals not only listen to differing points of view, they see events like the one in question as opportunities to put hard questions to conservatives. Second, if they canceled the event, they would miss out on an opportunity to hone their argumentation skills—skills that would be important to them in the future. Then he asked a difficult but pertinent question: "Do you just want to make noise or do you want to make progress?"

Denver told the student leaders, "I have confidence in you. You are smart students. Instead of protesting, why not demonstrate what freedom of speech really means? Research the subject the conservative politician is going to speak on, attend his speech, and ask him some hard questions. Pin him down with hard facts and look for holes in his arguments. The concept is known as critical thinking—something I hope you will all learn before graduation. Any fool can get angry, make threats, and protest, but the wise individual knows a better way. Take my advice today, and someday in the future you will debate presidential candidates as I have. In fact, you might one day be a presidential candidate."

The meeting with their hero had not gone the way the radical student leaders hoped, but they had to admit his reasoning was sound and his advice good. They decided to take his advice. The students thoroughly researched the subject of the upcoming speech and, during the question-and-answer session, asked hard questions. The conservative speaker was well-versed on his topic and, therefore, able to answer their questions. At the end of his speech, he told the students how proud he was of them for demonstrating critical thinking and honoring freedom of speech. He said, "When I run for president, I would be proud to debate anyone of you or to have you on my side of the debate." As a result of Denver's advice, a potential riot turned into a good learning experience.

BIBLICAL TRUTHS ABOUT LIES ON THE INTERNET

The internet was not even developed when the Bible was written (though the Lord already knew about it), but lying, distorting, deceiving, and spreading propaganda were very much a part of life during Jesus's time on earth. If you use the internet or social media, expect that much of what you read is posted for the purpose of deception and distortion. In other words, those who posted the information are lying.

Lying on the internet is no different than lying in person except on the internet or social media the lie spreads to a larger audience in a matter of minutes. People who go online should be cautious. Never accept anything off the internet without thoroughly investigating its provenance and reliability. The Bible speaks to this advice in Luke 12:2 where we are assured nothing is hidden that will not be revealed. In other words, the truth will eventually rise to the surface. The Bible also tells us the naïve believe anything but the prudent give thought to their steps (Proverbs 14:15). This means we should be critical thinkers.

The Bible is clear about where it stands on lying, whether online or in person. In Zechariah 8:16–17, we are told to speak the truth to each other. Exodus 23:1 warns against spreading false reports. In Jeremiah 28, the prophet stands up to those who were spreading falsitys. This chapter in the Bible is edifying and worth your time to read. It is also worth considering the original falsity when Satan told Eve that she and Adam would not die if they ate the forbidden fruit (Genesis 3:4–5). Lying is nothing new. The internet has just made it easier and more pervasive.

BIBLICAL TRUTHS ABOUT THINKING OBJECTIVELY

Critical thinking helps us verify doctrines of the Christian faith are based in Scripture and on valid information. Critical thinking is critical to Christians because so many people try to distort what Scripture says for their own benefit. There is an important message in 1 John 4:1 on critical thinking. John warns us to avoid believing anything without testing it. Proverbs 4:23 tells us to be careful of what and how we think because our lives are shaped by our thoughts.

Since the Bible is clear about the expectation of Christians on this subject, no one should be afraid to be a critical thinker. Isaiah 41:10 tells us not to fear for God is with us and He will strengthen and help us. Matthew 6:25–33 tells us to be strong and fear nothing because God will come and save us. God's answer to our fears is prayer. In Philippians 4:6 He tells us to worry about nothing but to pray about everything. Fear is overcome through faith, which is complete trust in God. Trust in God and think objectively and your life will change for the better.

SUMMARY

- The Bible has much to say about critical thinking and the various skills that go with it. The only real, immutable, and accurate source of truth is Holy Scripture. God gave us His Word so we can know the truth. Critical thinking allows people to measure the validity of claims, assertions, ideas, and proposals against the truths found in the Bible. Biblical truths stand up to even the most aggressive arguments and the most detailed questions. This is why Christians who are critical thinkers are not afraid to be asked hard questions. The Bible gives them solid, irrefutable answers.
- All the critical thinking skills explained in this book have a biblical foundation including recognizing bias, human

motives, rationalizations, the need for research, short-term expedients, separating facts from opinions, applying common sense, responding to ad hominem attacks, standing up to the cancel culture, recognizing oversimplification, recognizing when people are avoiding inconvenient truths and uncomfortable facts, recognizing distorted conclusions, arguing productively, and recognizing lies on the internet.

OTHER BOOKS FROM OLIVER NORTH

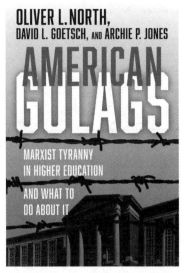

American Gulags: Marxist Tyranny in
Higher Education and What to Do About It
9781956454062—$20 / 9781956454079 eBook—$9.99

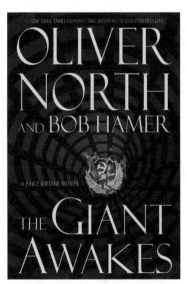

The Giant Awakes: A Jake Kruse Novel
9781956454048—$28 / 9781956454055 eBook—$12.99

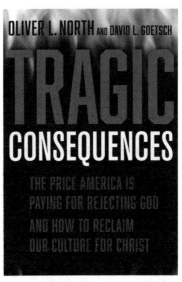

Tragic Consequences: The Price America is Paying for Rejecting God and How to Reclaim Our Culture for Christ

9781956454000—$28 / 9781956454017 eBook—$12.99

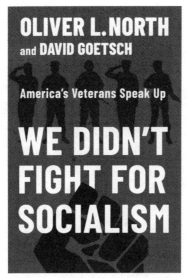

We Didn't Fight for Socialism: America's Veterans Speak Up

9781735856346—$26 / 9781735856353 eBook—$9.99